HOW TO EAT HUMBLE PIE
& Not Get Indigestion

Other Books by
Charlene Ann Baumbich

Don't Miss Your Kids!
(They'll be gone before you know it)

Mama Said There'd be Days Like This
(But she never said just how many)

The 12 Dazes of Christmas
(& One Holy Night)

The Book of DUH!
Celebrating those Less-then-magic Moments

HOW TO EAT HUMBLE PIE
& Not Get Indigestion

Charlene Ann Baumbich

Arbor Hill Press
Naperville, Illinois 60565

Cover illustration: Tim Nyberg

ISBN 1-890156-00-0

Second Edition

Printed in the United States of America.

Library of Congress Cataloging-in-Publication Data

Baumbich, Charlene Ann, 1945-
   How to eat humble pie and not get indigestion / Charlene Ann Baumbich.
      p.   cm.
   Includes bibliographical references.
   ISBN 1-890156-00-0
   1. Humility — Christianity. 2. Christian life — 1960- I. Title.
BV4647.H8B28   1993
241'.4—dc20   97-71868
                                                          CIP

97 98 99 00 01 02 03 04 05 / 15 14 13 12 11 10 9 8 7 6 5 4

Acknowledgments

By the time one is done writing a book about humility, one truly understands that nothing worthy gets accomplished without the energy, time, criticism and encouragement of others. Each person whom God ushers into our lives, whether it be by the written or spoken word or by quiet example, ultimately affects what comes out of us. This book is a by-product of the thoughts, voices and spirits of many.

Thanks to my parents who taught me the value of telling the truth about ourselves—even when the truth is totally humiliating. They showed me through example how to laugh about it, learn from it, heal and quickly move on.

Thanks to my friends who not only encouraged me but held me accountable; kindred spirits who were willing to share their stories and whose hearts were attuned to my passion, task and message; friends in the body of Christ who helped me see and then believe that light, God's light, can illuminate even the darkest blackness.

Thanks to Pat Colander who, way back when, not only allowed me to find my writing voice but also liked *and* paid for it!

Thanks to Pastor Rodney Broker who shared in lengthy conversations about humility and took the time to read my manuscript. (P.S. Extra-special thanks for *liking* it!)

Thanks to Al and Barb Unger not only for sustaining friendship but also for turning over the keys to their peaceful home on Lake Wisconsin so I could lock myself away to corral this project.

Thanks to the participants in the writers' workshops I attend: the Arbor Hill poetry gang for continuing to uphold the importance of every word *and* for giving me such a grand birthday party; and the El Torito gang (a.k.a. The Brain Deads) whose members share their professional knowledge and conduct superb whining sessions that ultimately yet joyfully exhaust us.

A special thanks to Gary Bradshaw who gave me permission to reprint large portions of an article he wrote about his daughter, an unequaled word picture that unfolds humility in action.

Thanks to everyone at InterVarsity Press, especially Don Stephenson who believed I could write this book even when I didn't; Rodney Clapp who calmed my hysteria; Linda Doll and Ruth Goring Stewart who put order to my text when it was necessary and deleted text that wasn't (and patiently listened to my arguments concerning the latter).

Thanks to sons Bret and Brian who keep me humble—in a number of ways!

Thanks to George (a.k.a. Basement Man), my dearly beloved husband, who, with great humility and personal sacrifice, allows his often crazed and selfish wife to chase her dreams.

Preface: Open to the Shining

For many weeks after I signed the contract to write this book, fear kept me from beginning. "Unqualified to write about humility" seemed a gross understatement, and not one ounce short of the truth. Were it not for the wise, inspired and encouraging words of others, I might have never been able to push through that fear. Madeleine L'Engle was a special help:

In a very real sense not one of us is qualified, but it seems that God continually chooses the most unqualified to do his work, to bear his glory. If we are qualified, we tend to think that we have done the job ourselves. If we are forced to accept our evident lack of qualification, then there's no danger that we will confuse God's work with our own, or God's glory with our own.[1]

Writing this book has been quite a journey. I began with some stories I wanted to tell; but during the months of writing, others' stories that were brought to me, and many stories that happened to me in that same period, left me amazed and filled with awe. It was as though God, with his quirky sense of humor, said, "Don't worry, child. I'll make sure you don't lack for material while you're writing about humility. I will feed you. I will feed you holy humble pies you never dreamed of. I will bring you stories of nearly unspeakable love. I AM is all the qualification you need. Just keep your eyes on me."

I hadn't dreamed how many blessings God would shower upon me through the research, the stories, and the house on Lake Wisconsin that my friends Al and Barb loaned me for three one-week stretches of writing. There were many points when I couldn't wait to see what was going to happen next, what wondrous thing God would open up to me through the process. I am still taking it in; I hope I never forget it.

There were times when I had many more questions than answers—and I still do. You will see a variety of those questions on these pages. But I have learned that questions are okay; humility knows that. God has the answers, and it's not my job to try and sort them all out. I just need to keep listening.

Reuben Welch writes in *We Really Do Need Each Other:*

If God is light means God shines, then for me to walk in the light means for me to walk in the shining of God. The best way I know how to think of it is this: God shines in Jesus and when I am walking in the light, I am walking

with the roof of my life open to the shining of God. I
understand that kind of mental image—to walk in the light
means to take the roof off, open up the ceiling, and let the
Son shine in.[2]

In my writing I've hoped simply to be open to the shining,
so that God's light could pour through to you.

1

The
Thirst

ONCE upon a hot summer's Fourth of July, Charlene and her son Brian followed the end of the grand hometown parade into the park where festivities were to continue. George, Charlene's husband, said he would make the long walk to the car and pick them up in front of the park. In the meantime, Charlene and Brian could check out the celebration to see whether they'd want to come back later in the day.

Someone was announcing over the P.A. that the pie-eating contest was going to begin, and anyone six years old and under should come up to the trailer if they wanted to participate. The emcee said that older kids would be called up next.

"Brian, why don't you compete?" Charlene tossed out a

challenge to her junior-high-age son.

"Get serious!" he said.

"Come on. Haven't you ever wanted to just stick your face in a pie? What an opportunity!"

"No way."

"Bri. I think you're chicken."

"Mom, I'm not chicken; but I'm also not stupid!"

"Brian, being willing to get a little pie on your face doesn't mean you're stupid. It means you're willing to have fun and take risks. I think it would really be fun. Look, it's those little pies you like anyway. The little packaged ones that they sell in your lunchroom."

"So?"

"So, go for it. Come on. Have some guts!"

"No."

This discussion went on all throughout the under-six-years-of-age contest. Mother and son saw that contestants had to hold their hands behind their backs while eating the pie out of the tin. First one done was the winner. The tricky part, of course, was that the pie kept slipping around the table because of its tin, and it was quite amusing to watch the little kids chasing these skittering miniature pies around with their mouths.

At any rate, George hadn't arrived with the car yet, and it was entertaining, so Charlene and Brian hung around in the shade to watch, leaning on a tree. When Brian's age bracket came up, Charlene made one last attempt at persuading her stubborn son to join in this wonderful fun, but he refused.

Just as Charlene and Brian were beginning to head toward the curb to wait for George, assuming the contest was over, the emcee announced that there was going to be a sixteen-

and-over competition. Charlene paid no attention to this announcement, but Brian perked up his ears.

"Mom! There's your chance! Get up there." ("Up there" was the trailer being used for an announcement booth and competitors' platform.)

"Brian, your dad will be here in a minute. Besides, this is for kids."

"Mom, they said sixteen and over. You're definitely over sixteen. You told me how wonderful it was, so what's your excuse? Are you chicken?"

That did it. Charlene, before engaging her brain, set her body in motion toward the trailer. Next thing she knew, she was up on the stage with four other contestants—all of whom were barely over sixteen. Looking out into the crowd, Charlene decided maybe this wasn't such a hot idea, but what the heck, she was already up there. Besides that, her competitive spirit surged inside her—although it never needs much coaxing. She had a plan.

"Get ready, get set, *go!*"

With the agility and cleverness of the most agile and clever, Charlene kicked her plan into gear. Remember, she had noticed that the hard part was chasing the tin around the table; so she quickly *got the pie out of the tin!* This strategy was nothing short of brilliant. In one motion, Charlene picked up the tin with her teeth and flipped the pie out onto the paper. She then took a deep breath, opened wide her jaws and nearly inhaled the entire mini-pie with one swoop, simultaneously standing up in triumph and raising her hands high over her head. The winning grin was a little more difficult to manage because her mouth was stuffed with pie, but she didn't care.

Victory is sweet—for a flash, at least.

The crowd cheered. "Did you see that?" they said. "What a move!" "How clever." Charlene relished the victory, quickly scanning the table and noticing that nary a bite had been taken out of any of the other pies. Ah, what a clever competitor she was.

Then it hit her. Charlene was standing in front of a crowd in the midst of teenage competitors with her mouth full of pie she couldn't swallow and the remnants stuck all over her face. About this time, a reporter from the local newspaper came to get her name.

This, dear readers, is literal pie in the face.

Although her ribbon hangs proudly in her office, and she has to admit the entire episode was fun and exhilarating— and it's encouraging that she, a midlifer, can still spontaneously go for it—the phone calls that arrived after the newspaper article was published were nearly as humiliating as that moment when she stood like a pie-smeared idiot in front of the crowd—and the reporter.

"That isn't really you who won the pie-eating contest, is it?"

Now I ask, how many people named Charlene Ann Baumbich do you know?

* * *

Literal pie in the face; a symbolic holy pie in the face. Sometimes it's hard to tell the difference. They have the potential to deliver equal doses of humility; they splat into our lives with surprising force; we've usually asked for them.

Either one can be a moment that eradicates pride, if you're willing to let it. A moment that draws you closer to the bosom of the Lord, if you're willing to learn from his playful attention-getter rather than simply whining about the mess.

Sadly enough, it usually takes gazillions of bouts of pie-smeared humiliating moments before we discover this truth: Humble pie is a holy feast.

As I mentally survey my past, it seems to be four and a half decades lived in varying degrees of self-importance. Only God's awesome power could penetrate this bundle of pride. Only God's awesome power could make me *want* my pride deflated.

If you had told me five years ago that I would thirst to explore and write about humility, I would have thrown up the crossed-finger symbol they use to keep Dracula away.

"Sheesh! How boring and dull," I would have snapped. After all, I've been told I have panache (although I had to run home and look that word up) and that I dress with eclectic style (don't wear things that match); and I consider myself quite the passionate and gregarious type. I love my Lord, and know his love for me. Isn't that enough?

Humility? That's for Mother Teresa and people who might find flogging themselves a treat. Not us happening folk who, most of the time, seem to have our dynamic Christian acts together—at least on the outside.

Of course it would not be fair to say I never experienced humility in my pre-thirst days. I must admit to bursts—attacks, you might say—of humility. The mother of two grown boys, I experienced innumerable humbling moments through the child-rearing years. In fact, recalling several of those episodes inspired me to write a chapter about humility in my last book, *Don't Miss Your Kids! (They'll Be Gone Before You Know It)*. The chapter was called "Learning to Eat

Crow," and that pretty much says it all. There's nothing like children to bring you to your knees!

As for my life aside from parenting, there have been hundreds, thousands even, of embarrassing escapades and overwhelmingly grand moments that have prompted bursts of humility: spectacular sunsets, wipeouts on the ski slopes, a speeding ticket, watching a birth . . . cliché images, really. We all have many such moments. Beauty to behold, misery to plow through. Humiliations that don't seem to matter much after a day or two. Blessings we take for granted.

Though the sense of awe and humility I experienced at such moments generally wore off quickly, gradually things began to change in me. No, not my style of clothes or upbeat attitude. May that never be! It was more like an awakening. A slow, stretching, muscle-by-muscle move into a new realm: the realm of humility. Truly desiring to become the humble person Christ calls me to be. Wanting to move pride aside and allow the glory of Christ within me to shine.

Through an ongoing and (usually) gentle nudging of the Holy Spirit, I began to realize the awesome grace of God. I began to understand that less of me allowed more of him. I began to enter the *rest* of knowing that apart from God I can do nothing of eternal value, yet he can do it all through me. I began to experience the peace and joy that linger only in oneness with the Lord.

I hadn't thought I needed this. God slowly revealed to me, however, that I could walk into an enveloping, comforting, joy-filled freedom beyond anything I'd known—if only I could become humble.

I spent hours poring over the Scriptures. And I found no

surprises. I found only validations.

Take my yoke upon you and learn from me, for I am gentle and humble in heart, and you will find rest for your souls. For my yoke is easy and my burden is light. (Mt 11:29-30) All of you, clothe yourselves with humility toward one another, because "God opposes the proud but gives grace to the humble." Humble yourselves, therefore, under God's mighty hand, that he may lift you up in due time. (1 Pet 5:5-6)

He has showed you, O man, what is good. And what does the LORD require of you? To act justly and to love mercy and to walk humbly with your God. (Mic 6:8)

The thirst awakened. I set out to make myself humble.

Bad idea! Every deliberate humbling action on my part led to the awareness of more pride. I slammed smack into myself around every self-serving corner, even though at first I believed my actions were sincere attempts to humble myself. In an odd way, of course, they were. Problem was, I, Me, Self, was trying to do it alone. I was trying to conquer Me with my power and might.

But my Spirit-driven thirst did not wane. It was not easily quenched or dissuaded. It grew ever stronger. And through thirst, prayer and sincere desire, God, not I, began to reveal to me that humility is essential to the fulfilled Christian life. A creative life that honors my God-given uniqueness, my individual way to reflect his glory (2 Cor 3:18).

These revelations in my life were flashes of heaven; I can think of no other way to put it. For the first time, it seemed that it might actually be okay to be me. After all, I was God's workmanship (Eph 2:10).

I wanted to explore the topic further. So I enthusiastically went to Christian bookstores to learn more about this revelation. I even thought that someday I might write about it.

"Where are your books on the topic of humility?" I asked. And time after time I was greeted with the same message. "Gee, there don't seem to be many specifically on that topic. After all, who would dare write about it?"

Yikes! Spiritual whiplash. I can't think of another way to describe what those words did to me. Who was I to dare?

At first I believed I was receiving another in the string of holy pies in the face that God often uses to encourage me to get "on line." *Get real, Charlene. Give it up. Leave this one to scholars and saints.*

I would bring the topic up with friends, Christian friends, who either became uncomfortable or laughed at me.

"Charlene, people cannot become humble," I heard time and time again. "The more you try, the worse it will get. And if you can finally say, 'I am humble,' you can bet you're not!" Hm. Food for thought.

But I remembered the Scriptures I'd read. And if Christ requires our humility, surely he will empower us to become humble. Otherwise, he would be a sadistic sort, wouldn't he? And we know better than to believe that!

So why did some people react so negatively when I tried to talk about something so beautiful? Why had I myself balked at humility so strongly?

I have come to believe there are many misunderstandings about what it means to be a humble person. I'm convinced that many people skirt the topic because (1) they believe humility is unobtainable, or (2) they are afraid that exploring the biblical theme of humility would bring uncomfortable conviction, or (3) they are afraid that if they did embrace humility, they would become either boring, unpopular dweebs or replicas of the Church Lady on "Saturday Night Live"—or something worse. I myself have uncritically accepted all three of these mistaken assumptions, and others too.

Now, however, I hold humility in the highest regard. Through holy pies in the face—those embarrassing or awe-filled moments I spoke of before—God has blessed me with some of the sweet fruits of humility. These pies and their lessons have come in many forms, from mincemeat that left me picking off the gooey remnants for years afterward, to whipped-cream pies whose soft, sweet flecks I licked off my lips and swallowed deep into my hungering, searching soul.

"The Christian life has suffered loss," Andrew Murray says in his classic book *Humility,* "because believers have not been distinctly guided to see that nothing is more natural and beautiful and blessed than to be nothing, so that God may be all.

"If we are indeed to be humble, not only before God but toward men—if humility is to be our joy—we must see that it is not just viewed as the mark of shame because of sin. It must also be understood apart from all sin as a covering with the very beauty and blessedness of heaven and of Jesus."[1]

Murray cautions us to avoid becoming caught up in "qualifications and limitations, so many reasonings and questionings" about what humility really is that we give up seeking it. I suspect that fear underlies our initial reactions to the topic—a fear that needs to be overcome if we are to experience God's fullest blessings.

* * *

Humility. There's a lot to it. And the more God reveals its intricacies, the more I am left wanting more. I've always been the kind of person who wants *more.* But perhaps this greedy, thirsty characteristic won't turn out so bad in the end if I keep it pointed in the right direction: off my own selfish needs and upwards to God's shining face.

I think of the thirst Christ expressed before his death.

He hung on a cross, giving himself for us. Tired, beaten, dying. And in order that the Scripture might be fulfilled, he said, "I am thirsty."

"I am thirsty." Whenever I read this part of the story, a picture of my grandfather comes to mind. It was 1959; I was fourteen years old. I saw my grandfather—my kind, laughter-filled, twinkly-eyed grandfather—tired, beaten by cancer of the esophagus, dying. In the very end, he was barely able to speak his thirst.

I watched my grandmother dip the edge of a soft cloth into a cool, fresh bowl of water and gently touch the precious moisture to Grandpa's parched lips. And soon it was finished. Grandpa was gone.

I cannot honestly say what happened to my grandfather's soul when he died. I would like to believe that it went up to be with Christ. I do not know.

The Bible tells us that when Christ spoke of his thirst, someone ran and got a sponge, filled it with wine vinegar, put it on a stick and offered it to him to drink. And, John tells us, "when he had received the drink, Jesus said, 'It is finished.' With that, he bowed his head and gave up his spirit" (Jn 19:30).

Isn't it curious that he spoke of thirst? That he said, "I am thirsty"? Isn't it odd that a man who spent his days convincing others that they need thirst no more—King Thirst Quencher, you might say—would end his earthly life speaking of his own thirst? Listen now to some of his promises.

When the woman at the well asked Jesus why he, a Jew, would ask a Samaritan woman for a drink, he said, "If you knew the gift of God and who it is that asks you for a drink, you would have asked him and he would have given you living water." He went on to say, "Everyone who drinks this water [from the well] will be thirsty again, but whoever drinks the water I give him will never thirst. Indeed, the water I give him will become in him a spring of water welling up to eternal life." And the woman said to him, "Sir, give me this water so that I won't get thirsty," and he did (Jn 4:10, 13-15).

Just a few chapters later, John tells us, "on the last and greatest day of the Feast, Jesus stood and said in a loud voice, 'If anyone is thirsty, let him come to me and drink. Whoever believes in me, as the Scripture has said, streams of living water will flow from within him' " (Jn 7:37-38). Time after time, Christ promised his people they would thirst no more.

Before God sent his Son to us to tell us about the living water, God often quenched his people's physical thirst. He made water flow from a rock; he made rivers flow on barren heights and springs within valleys. He even quenched the thirst of the wild donkeys. Psalm 107 tells us the Lord has satisfied the thirsty soul. Isn't it odd, then, that Christ, who quenched thirst, and who was begotten of God, who quenches thirst, spoke of his own thirst at the end?

Perhaps, just maybe, his was the same thirst David spoke of in Psalm 42. "As the deer pants for streams of water, so my soul pants for you, O God. My soul thirsts for God, for the living God. When can I go and meet with God?" (vv. 1-2).

Christ hung on the cross and said, "I am thirsty." Perhaps he didn't say it because his throat was dry. Perhaps his thirst was the same as David's: *to be with his heavenly Father.* And having said this, he died. He was buried, resurrected and taken up into heaven where he sat at the right hand of God (Mk 16:19).

Perhaps he used some of his last precious breath to show us that when we cry out to our Lord because our souls are thirsty, he will, indeed, fill us with living water—the water of the Holy Spirit. And we, like Christ, shall be forever united in oneness with our God.

Perhaps my grandfather's words of thirst were far more meaningful than I imagined. I can only hope. But what we can know beyond a shadow of a doubt is that God quenches our thirst, if only we ask. He promised.

* * *

And so Charlene takes her thirst and bravely enters the vast and beckoning galaxies of humility. Come with me on my journey, but fasten your seat belt; it's bound to be a bumpy ride.

If you're already an expert at being humble, or if you're not really convinced humility is all I'm making it out to be, come along anyway. At the very least, as you're reading along you'll probably think of somebody else who needs to learn about humility.

That's what one of my more encouraging friends said: "Everybody will know *somebody* they'll want to give this book to! Everybody knows somebody who needs a good dose of humility." And then we both laughed.

2

What
Humility
Is Not

ABOUT a year ago I mentioned to a friend that I had been thinking a lot about humility. She almost snapped my head off.

"It's taken me twelve years to gain my sense of self-esteem. Don't go throwing your humility thoughts" (actually, this wasn't the phrase she used) "at me!" Our casual phone conversation had suddenly taken a wrong turn.

"What did you think I was going to say?" I asked her rather quietly, having been thrown on the defensive by her tongue-lashing.

"Nobody needs to be a doormat," she spat. "Nobody needs to let the world run over them."

I was stunned. What a rebuke! My mind reeled. After all, my experience with God had recently led me to begin concluding that perhaps humility was the key to happiness. Oh, not that I'd actually *become* a humble person by any means. Goodness no. It wasn't that long ago that some friends in my scratch bowling league affectionately dubbed me Char the Star—a title that I not only enjoyed (and still do) but claimed. I even purchased a star charm to wear on a silver chain.

"Doormat? Is that what you think I was going to say?" I finally squeaked into the receiver. "Is that what you think God means when he calls us to be humble? A doormat?"

I had forgotten that some people thought feeling good about yourself was in conflict with humility. It hadn't occurred to me that letting every thoughtless person in the world walk all over you was humility.

One of two things was the case here: either my friend, my Christian friend, was wrong, or I needed to take another look at my position.

Our phone conversation quickly degenerated into a sort of wary dance: my friend's self-protection from what she perceived as an attack, mingled with her apologies for snapping; I in turn apologizing for obviously hitting a sore spot, but still trying to protect my fledgling, as-yet-undeveloped theory on humility—that it is a means to freedom and grace. I quickly realized that I couldn't sufficiently defend my position.

Actually, it wasn't really a position yet. It was more like a link in a chain of events that God long ago began in my life. I needed more proof. More Scriptures on the tip of my tongue. More pondering. More discussions. More examples of this humility-joy connection played out in my life. As usual, I needed more of everything. Not a very humble quality, I suspected.

Since that phone conversation, however, much of my time has been spent seeking the "more" I felt was lacking. Although I am far from having all the answers, and my journey to become the humble person Christ calls me to be is far from ended, I have become more convinced than ever that humility is the key to all that is good, beginning with Christ's humble, obedient gift of salvation.

* * *

The main problem with humility is that it isn't what so many people think it is. There—I've said it! After all these months and years, after all my hard, sometimes anguished study of the topic, I can finally say with resolution why people don't like to think or talk about humility: it isn't what they think it is.

They think it means less, not more. They consider it comparable to being a *doormat* that everyone steps on rather than a *doorway* through which God himself enters to fill you. They think . . . *wrong!*

Months ago I nearly jumped out of my pew during a sermon by the Reverend Dr. Rodney L. Broker, a.k.a. Rod (also called Friend), my pastor. I got so excited about it that I had him send me a copy of it. Then I put it away and promptly forgot where it was. Today I found it—in a folder labeled "False Humility." Who would have ever thought I'd been that organized so long ago?

Let me give a key to humility, right out of one of Friend Rod's sermons. A sermon called "Nobility Has Its Obligations." Thank you, Rod.

John proclaims that we belong to Christ the King. We belong to "him who loves us and has freed us from our sins by his blood, and has made us to be a kingdom and priests to serve his God and Father" (Rev 1:5-6). That is who we are, and that is what our lives are to be about.

One day during World War II, Brigadier General Teddy Roosevelt Jr. was waiting at the airport to catch a plane. A young soldier stepped up to the ticket window and said, "Please, I need to get home to my mother, and I don't have much time." The agent explained that there was no space available on the flight he needed. The soldier became quite upset.

Roosevelt saw and heard what was going on, so he stepped up to the agent and said, "Give this soldier my seat." A friend immediately questioned him, "But Teddy, aren't you in a hurry too?" And Roosevelt replied, "Yes, but it's just a matter of rank. I'm only a general. He is . . . a son!"

That's what the Bible says about you and me. We are heirs to the Kingdom of the Most High God. We are nobility. The tragedy is not that we think too much of ourselves, but that we think too little.

Bingo! We think humility will make us *too little.* The world has brainwashed us into believing that the humble get trampled. Most people don't understand that true humility, not false humility, is strength and power and Spirit-guided direction. Humility is *all,* not nothing. Humility is not self-abasement; it's boasting in who we are: children of the Almighty God.

Self-esteem is nothing compared to Christ-in-me knowledge. "For it is God who is at work within you, giving you the will and the power to achieve his purpose" (Phil 2:13 Phillips).

And in the light of this grace we perceive the power of grace in our relation to ourselves. We experience moments in which we accept ourselves, because we feel that we have been accepted by that which is greater than we. If only more such moments were given to us! For it is such moments that make us love our life, that make us accept ourselves, not in our goodness and self-complacency, but in our certainty of the eternal meaning of our life.[1]

* * *

False humility lurks around every corner, however, trying to lure us away from what is best. To lull us into believing that humility means "worthless," not "royal."

Pride deceives us into believing that our efforts—works— can handle any and everything. Pride stops humility dead in its tracks and we don't even realize it. We are totally deceived.

Case in point: Not long after I signed the contract with InterVarsity Press to write about humility, an editor I've worked with at another company said, "I prayed for humility once six years ago. Never again! It was the worst period of my life."

My guess is that this person never once began to get a glimpse of what true humility was. All he saw was what it wasn't. Too bad. The fact that he prayed for it leads me to believe that he genuinely wants to please God. But pride deceived him into believing that humility equaled one rotten thing after another. What he doesn't understand is that humility isn't a matter of getting something; it's an issue of surrender. And surrender is different from commitment. "Commitment is what I am promising to do for God. Surrender is placing myself and my life in His hands to do with as He pleases."[2]

My guess is that this editor's own pride grabbed hold of every holy pie that smacked him in the face and rebelled against it. Humility, on the other hand, welcomes the pie and stays for the clean-up. Humble folks allow Christ to wash them with warm waters until they are whiter than snow. True humility values the lessons. Humility transforms us, unveils us so that we reflect God's glory—but only when pride is set aside.

God does humble the proud. And lessons and difficulties do often come in strings. But a vow never to pray for humility again—? I fear what it might take for my editor friend to learn to see humility in a new light. Of course the beautiful part—and the most humbling to me in pondering this—is that God loves him endlessly. Just as he loves all the rest of his children. Just as he loves Char the Star during each of her pride-filled enterprises and each of her unsubmissive spells and each of her bouts of judging others when it's her own eye she ought to be examining just in case she might find an entire forest growing there. And far too often she does.

For the friend who hated the idea of this book, for my editor friend, for yourself, for myself, let's look now at false humility in its many guises. My guess is that this exploration will be alternately reassuring and convicting for you, just as it has been for me.

Martyrdom

Now hear this: Martyrdom is not humility. Getting on every committee at church, leading two Bible studies, volunteering for countless other "good works," getting by on four hours of sleep per night, taking in your neighbor's laundry . . . and then running around exhausted because you have overextended and thoroughly depleted yourself *is not humility*. It is functioning in pure works. No grace. No faith. No fun. Pure works.

God asks no one to do it all. Not even Moses. Exodus 18 tells us how Moses was sitting from morning until evening as a judge. All the Israelites brought him their differences to solve. Finally, one day his father-in-law said to him, "What is this you are doing for the people? Why do you alone sit as judge, while all these people stand around you from morning till evening?"

Moses responded, "The people come to me to seek God's will." He felt responsible to apply God's laws to their many problems.

But Moses' father-in-law warned, "What you are doing is not good. You and these people who come to you will only wear yourselves out. The work is too heavy for you; you cannot handle it alone. Listen now to me and I will give you some advice, and may God be with you." Jethro went on to explain to Moses that he should teach others the decrees and laws and show them how to perform the duties of a leader. Train others. Let them decide simple matters themselves. Share the load. "If you do this and God so commands, you will be able to stand the strain, and all these people will go home satisfied" (Ex 18:13-23).

Angel Jethro—from the camp of the in-laws, no less!

Trying to do it all not only exhausts you but keeps others from growth and the opportunity to use their gifts. And, in any case, God does not call you to be a superperformer. He calls you to peace and faithfulness.

Pathetics

Sometimes people see humility as a pathetic condition. Jim Conway refers to these folks as "the pathetics." I know I've fallen into this category on occasion. In fact, it's easy to start thriving, in some peculiar way, as a pathetic if one is not careful. Conway says,

These people irritate me. Yet at the same time I feel sorry for them. Maybe the reason they irritate me is because I feel guilty. I feel as if I ought to help them, but then I get mad at myself for being manipulated by them. Sometimes I'm part of the problem that keeps them dependent because I always jump to their aid.

Pathetic people whine, they complain a lot. Frequently they talk about life with great resignation: "Well, it just never works out for me." Often, you'll hear them sigh, "Oh, I don't know," or they repeatedly take deep breaths.

Many of these people don't even realize they are doing these things. They have learned that if they act pathetic, people will reach out and give them love. They don't believe they're lovable on their own, so they create or expand a problem to get others to love them.[3]

Pathetics underestimate who they are. Humility is not retreating from life under cover of our pathetic weakness. It is stepping forward *in God's strength.*

True humility also helps us respond appropriately to pathetics. Like Moses when he did things for others that he could teach them to do themselves, sometimes we're part of the problem that keeps them dependent, pathetic. We want to fix their lives for them.

Yes, true humility does want to serve. But we need to be ever careful about our motives. Overzealousness to "help" can do more harm than good.

Hypocrisy

I don't really need to say that hypocrisy is definitely not humility. Hypocrisy is false humility wearing its best mask. Hypocrisy is what usually gets nonbelievers especially angry at us Christians. Hypocrisy works against witnessing and therefore is a grave sorrow to God as much as a sin. I need say no more.

Faces of Gloom

"Faces of gloom" differ from the pathetics in that the gloomies look gloomy on purpose. Because they want to. They equate looking gloomy with looking spiritual. Chuck Swindoll says,

> Have you ever been around people who really wanted to look spiritual? They are gloom personified, apparently living out one of the unwritten laws in the ancient code of pharisaical ethics. Down through the centuries of Christianity many have cultivated that "seriously religious" appearance. It is especially popular among superpious missionaries who talk about the burden of the mission field, or among pastors who are weighted down with the burden

of the pastorate. Burden? Whose burden? The ministry is His burden. Since that is true, what are we doing bearing His burden and trying to look so grim about it? We ought to be grim if we are attempting to carry what God is supposed to carry! But we are not made to carry out His role, so let's stop trying. Playing a false role promotes pride, which is easily detected.[4]

Whoops! Gotcha. How easily the gloomy face ends up looking like and actually becoming a form of pride. What an interesting thought—and warning. And it all began with a servant's wanting to look humble while carrying God's job. Whew! All the more reason to take the "fun" part of humility more seriously. (I'm taking it so seriously that I'm devoting a whole chapter of this book to it.)

Flogging

Contrary to the way many of us Christians act much of the time, flogging ourselves is not humility. Flogging ourselves and walking around guilty, guilty, guilty denies the blood Christ shed to free us from guilt. I simply cannot believe that God sacrificed his only Son so that we could walk around stooped and miserable over our rottenness.

If ever I was caught up in a case of false humility, it was when I kept asking the question: Who am I to write about humility? I am such a miserable wretch. Oh, undeserving, undesirable, unworthy, unhumble me.

Yuck! Who wants to listen to that? I tell you this: Many of my friends had to as I walked through the fear of facing this task.

As I finally understood: Who am I _not_ to write about

God's design for us? Not one person who penned a story in the Bible was sin-free. Did that keep them from becoming vessels for God's holy Word?

Now don't get me wrong. I am not professing to be adding to God's holy Word by writing this book. But you know, it's my desire and my hope and my mission to serve the One who created me for his good works. And certainly I can't do that if I'm walking around flogging myself instead of spreading the good news.

So I accept Christ's good work on my behalf and stop flogging myself. That's the humblest thing I can do.

Silence

Silence is a blessed condition. It can also be deceptive.

I spent long periods during my growing-up years immersed in silence. I was raised on a small farm. Even as I type this I can close my eyes and see the beams of light that pierce the darkness of my beloved big white barn. I can smell the straw and hay, the leather tack hanging by the stalls. I hear the pigeons flapping their wings and cooing. I can feel the warmth of a colt as I wrap my arms around it. The silence of sitting in the upper doorway with my legs dangling as I watch the mares and foals romp and graze in the field.

Those who know me now will find my love of silence hard to fathom. Impossible perhaps. I am not often in another's company without talking. A lot. Fast. But silence comes very naturally to me when I am alone. I love being where there is no television, no radio and no telephone. Although those things are available to me at the lakeside house where I've been writing, I choose to deny them, aside from a daily phone call to my husband, a couple of necessary work calls and a once-a-week touch-bases-with-a-friend encounter.

It was only when I began to come here that I realized how much energy I spend talking. How much longer I can work when I haven't expended all that energy talking. How focused thoughts can stay without interruption. How loud the still small voice inside me can speak when I'm not drowning it out with worldly noises—including my own.

Silence beckons me. I find it a difficult transition to reenter my home with the yapping dog and the phone calls that must be returned and the sounds of the garbage disposal and a husband who wants to talk when I'm not yet ready and . . .

Silence: alluring, beckoning, resting silence. Scriptural silence: "Be still, and know that I am God" (Ps 46:10).

Silence can also be a way to hide. Silence that can appear to be humility rather than a way to keep others at arm's length. That keeps our wounds buried and out of the healing light. That makes others, after a time, wonder what we are hiding.

One-word answers like "fine" and "okay" escape out of the depths of silence when we really are "gravely wounded from the sting of your words" or "worried sick about the pain I've had in my side for weeks now" or "lying awake each night, sobbing into my pillow with grief for people and places that are no longer in my life."

Sometimes grief and pain and sorrow and fear hide behind silence because we mistakenly believe that humility stoically keeps everything in.

Even Jesus wept when Lazarus died. The psalmists poured out their hearts to the Lord. Paul wrote about the agony of doing the very things that he hated to do. He and other biblical writers spoke of their pain and suffering.

But the good news always prevailed. And how can we tell about God's goodness in our lives if we don't acknowledge and share the burdens and sins that Christ has conquered? Silence needs to be broken so that others can see his power made strong in our weaknesses.

Silence is golden—but sometimes the gold is fake, a thin veneer of cheap metal. A deceptive false humility.

Blitherers Disease

Humorist Dave Barry got me nearly hysterical with laughter as I read one of his columns in which he referred to the two women seated in front of him on an airplane as afflicted with Blitherers Disease, "which occurs when there is no filter attached to the brain, so that every thought the victim has, no matter how minor, comes blurting right out." Actually, the two women didn't suffer; he did. And he didn't use the word *afflicted,* he simply said they "had" the disease. But *afflicted* seems to be a good word to tag on this disease.

Blitherers Disease is, of course, the opposite of silence, and I have often suffered bouts of it. As in "had" it. But what does Blitherers Disease have to do with false humility? you ask. Good question.

The answer is, Any of us can talk a good round of humility. We can, in fact, talk the entire subject right into the ground. We can pass on very faulty information about humility. We can be so filled with our wonderful humbling acts of kindness or pity or servanthood that we blither about it—out of pure pride!

There is no humility if you are bragging and blithering about it. There is humility if your spirit is filled with joy and you know what you know, and that is Jesus Christ. Amen.

Somewhere between silence and blithering we must seek balance. Appropriate, divine balance.

Slavery

False humility often appears more like slavery than servanthood. More like bondage than freedom. "So you are no longer a slave, but a son; and since you are a son, God has made you also an heir" (Gal 4:7). "It is for freedom that Christ has set us free. Stand firm, then, and do not let yourselves be burdened again by a yoke of slavery" (Gal 5:1). The NIV Study Bible notes say about the "yoke" in this text: "The burden of the rigorous demands of the law as the means for gaining God's favor—an intolerable burden for sinful man."

We are not slaves to sin or to the law. We are God's children. Freed. So let's act like it. Walking around like you have a ball and chain attached to your legs isn't humility; it's bad information. Going around preaching the letter of the law is not truth; it is crazy-making. And it comes from pride, not humility. Our focus should be not what we *shouldn't* do, but what we are free to do as we live under the shining of God's face.

If you are feeling like a slave, it's time for a false humility check. Somehow, somewhere, someplace, sometime, your trolley has slipped off the track.

* * *

If you're truly seeking humility, be prepared for all kinds of false starts. Lack of joy might be your first sign that you've taken a wrong turn.

If you are humble and repentant before God but never apologize to or forgive human beings, you are falsely humble. If you often find yourself saying, "I have no mercy for someone who acts like that," it's time to look at your own life. Those who show no mercy usually know no mercy. They are denying one of God's prolific gifts of grace. Only true humility receives mercy and passes it on. False humility does not act as a vessel; it sinks like a cement pontoon, weighted with its own pride.

False humility is no humility at all.

So what is *true* humility? Let me repeat: True humility is strength and power and Spirit-guided direction. Humility is peace and grins and freedom. Humility is all. Humility is boasting in who we are: children of the Almighty God.

3

Incentives

JUST in case you haven't gotten around to accepting God's little nudgings toward the desire to lead a humble life, let me toss you a couple of Scriptures that perhaps haven't crossed your path lately, or that you didn't visualize in living color when you read them.

In Exodus 10:3-6 God delivers a pretty graphic warning to Pharaoh on the topic.

So Moses and Aaron went to Pharaoh and said to him, "This is what the LORD, the God of the Hebrews, says: 'How long will you refuse to humble yourself before me?

Let my people go, so that they may worship me. If you refuse to let them go, I will bring locusts into your country tomorrow. They will cover the face of the ground so that it cannot be seen. They will devour what little you have left after the hail, including every tree that is growing in your fields. They will fill your houses and those of all your officials and all the Egyptians—something neither your fathers nor your forefathers have ever seen from the day they settled in this land till now.' "

But Pharaoh didn't humble himself, so God hardened his heart and so the locusts came. In force they came. Pretty intense lesson about the value of humility!

Now I'm not suggesting that flying creatures will become activated and invade your abode should you miss a humbling opportunity, but hey—this Scripture should at the very least give us pause.

On a more comforting note, in her book *Seeking God,* Joni Eareckson Tada points out that "God, if he were so inclined, could destroy you with His white-hot wrath; yet He has chosen to be kind and merciful. His amazing grace is enough to humble us."[1] God's mercy is indeed what has moved me toward humility.

The May 11 page of the perpetual calendar that sits atop the little TV in my kitchen has something positive to say about humility as well: "Yielding to the will of God (which I believe cannot happen without humility) is not bondage— it is blessing." The accompanying Scripture text is, "Commit your way to the Lord; trust in him and he will do this: He will make your righteousness shine like the dawn, the justice of your cause like the noonday sun" (Ps 37:5-6).[2]

Beats locusts by a megaton. Positive reinforcement, you might say.

Here's another let's-not-mince-our-message Scripture: "The fear of the LORD is the beginning of knowledge, but fools despise wisdom and discipline" (Prov 1:7). No doubletalk there; those who do not humble themselves with discipline are nothing short of fools. "And those who walk in pride he is able to humble" (Dan 4:37). Oh, don't I know!

* * *

George and I have been married for twenty-three years, and it never ceases to amaze me how pride, especially mine, can still stir up deep trouble. Such was the case before a recent vacation. I, with my own hard-earned money, which took many thousands of written words to procure, purchased The Vacation Airline Tickets. And let it be said that I felt quite pleased and prideful with myself, *and* I exuberantly let George know about it on more than one occasion. (Never mind the fact that it was God who gave me the talent and the opportunities to earn the money and the time to take the vacation; it was I who made the purchase.) I made the reservations on the telephone, with the understanding that the tickets would arrive by mail.

One day when I was shuffling through the mounds of paper that seem to breed in specific areas of our home—the kitchen table, on the counter next to the microwave and *on the end table next to George's chair*—I discovered the envelope containing the tickets. Up to that point, I had been unaware that they had arrived. The envelope was under some junk mail piled *on the table next to George's chair*.

This discovery was made while George was at work. Although I didn't run to the phone and call George to chastise him for being so totally careless with these tickets (which I'd purchased with my hard-earned money), I did carry on for quite some time to the dog and the bird about this atrocious carelessness on George's part. After all, the tickets could have easily been thrown out by accident with all the junk mail.

My Monday-morning discovery mobilized me to action: it was time to gather *all* the stacks of papers and go through them. And so I did. I made one large pile on the table; various smaller piles were started as necessary. There were things that needed to go upstairs to my office; things that needed to be read when time was available; things that needed to be put someplace for safekeeping (including the airline tickets); things that needed to go in the garbage; things that George needed to go through because I had no idea what in the world they were all about . . . You get the picture. The entire top of the kitchen table was covered with piles of papers. The day moved along; piles were disbursed.

At nearly the crack of dawn on Wednesday morning—I've always been an early riser—I decided that I should log our flight information on the calendar. Although I had long ago, in red ink, written "Oregon" and "Home" on the correct squares of my "James Herriott's Yorkshire" calendar, I had not yet put exact times along with them.

I reached between the pages of the calendar and removed the little collection of papers. Stuff like invitations to parties, newspaper clippings of sales, airline tickets—the documentation of anything that is marked on the calendar. Oddly, however, the tickets were not in this little wad of stuff. Weird. I had never put such things in any other place. I shuffled through the stack time and again, but to no avail.

A prickly little feeling started running up the back of my neck, and my heartbeat sped up a bit. I wasn't hysterical, however; probably I put the tickets in the wrong stack during my Monday sorting.

Bet they were in my office. Wrong. Bet they were on George's dresser in his stack. Wrong. Bet they were mixed in with the junk-mail catalogs in the pile of things to read when time was available. Wrong. Bet they were in with the bills in the wicker doodah in the cabinet. Wrong.

I began to get hysterical when a Monday-morning flashback started piercing my thoughts. I envisioned all the piles on the table, including the important pile: The Vacation Airline Tickets. I recalled delivering the other piles to their proper places around the house. I remembered picking up the pile of things that went in the garbage. I remembered talking to Nellie, my parakeet, later in the day and discovering that the pile that was supposed to be in the garbage was instead on the corner of the table. (Must have set it there last time I talked to Nellie on my way to the garbage.) I remembered picking the stack up and tossing it in the garbage. *I remembered that the airline tickets had been sitting on that corner of the table where the pile for the garbage had been carelessly tossed. I remembered that the garbage man had come yesterday morning.*

I was now officially hysterical.

I raced around the house, retracing my earlier search with such speed that Wonderdog Butch began barking. I retraced those steps so many times, in fact, that I was beginning to feel like a dog before it lies down to sleep—circling, circling, circling. Butch yapped at my heels all the while.

Another vision came to my mind: I had carried something out to the garbage on Tuesday morning, garbage day. George had already put the bulk of the garbage curbside and was long gone to work. I noticed that our white garbage bag, the one from the kitchen, had a hole in its side. Undoubtedly one of those ugly giant crows had done the damage; it didn't look like the handiwork of a crawling animal. I shoved the bits of garbage I'd brought out in the hole and mumbled to myself about the pesky critters. This was what I recalled.

Suddenly, in this moment of recollection, I wondered if the hole had been a peephole supplied by God. Perhaps the tickets had actually been poking out of the bag. Even though at that moment I had not been aware that they were missing, perhaps I should have been more in tune with the Master. (What a pride-filled thought to imagine that I would, or should, never miss a trick!)

Then a wilder speculation captured my imagination: Perhaps a crow had dislodged the tickets from the garbage bag because the envelope had become smeared with some tasty kitchen crumbs. Perhaps the crow had flown away with the tickets, then dropped them when it decided they weren't so tasty after all. This possibility actually prompted a search of the immediate neighborhood.

The old adage from Scripture "Pride goes before destruction" (Prov 16:18) was playing in my ears. If I hadn't had such a hissy over George's careless behavior, maybe this wouldn't have happened to me. Little Miss Haughty! Getting what you deserve, aren't you? Finally, though, I decided to get off that self-abasing kick and consider a plan of action.

Number one: Call the airlines. Maybe they replace lost tickets. Yes, they do. For a one-hundred-dollar fee. One hundred dollars I didn't have.

Number two: Don't ever tell George. Order new ones on the MasterCard if I have to; earn more money to pay for them. But don't ever tell George. (No humble confession in my thoughts!)

Number three: Call and find out where the garbage goes after it's picked up. After all, I can describe the item I need: a tall white kitchen bag with a yellow drawstring and a hole in the side. Maybe if it wasn't buried I could find it. I called our carrier and explained the situation. The woman took my street address and said she'd make a couple calls to find out if Truck Number 113 had dumped its load. This was an outside possibility if it had been a light garbage day, she said. I sat by my phone and waited.

Only about five minutes passed before she called to inform me that Truck Number 113 had, in fact, not yet dumped its load. She said she had radioed the driver and told him to head for the dump. She had also phoned the gate at the dump and told them that the truck was coming and so was I. She asked me if I had ever seen what comes out of a dump truck, and suggested that I wear rubber gloves. She warned me that the odds might not be too good for retrieval, but also admitted that stranger things had happened. She told me where the dump was; I recognized it as a mountain about five miles from my home.

Briefly, I reconsidered the whole idea. I wondered whether I'd be able to stomach what comes out of the back of a garbage truck, considering that it had been in there overnight and the weather had been quite warm. I began to get cold feet, wondering whether I could actually go through with this. Then I thought about my mother.

Although Mom had been gone sixteen years, her pioneering and near-fearless spirit came to mind. I thought about the time a fox fell through the window well into our basement on the farm and was going berserk. Mom shot it. I still have the photograph of Mom with a rifle in one hand and a fox dangling from the other, tears streaming down her face. A fox-pelt muff is among my prized possessions because it is cloaked with Mom's character.

Mom wouldn't have let a little thing like garbage stop her. And so I grabbed my rubber gloves and a rake and headed for the garbage mound.

Soon mine was the only passenger car in a line of giant garbage trucks waiting to pass through the gates. Directly behind the entrance was The Mountain. Trucks groaned their way up the graded roads and disappeared to the other side of this green, lush, inviting swell in the earth.

When it was my turn at the gate, I had to get out of my car to step up on the platform by the window; it was raised to accommodate drivers of tall trucks. The woman in the cubicle laughed and said, "You must be Charlene. Just pull up over there; the truck's on its way. Ernie will be with you in a minute."

Truck after truck rumbled by me, their drivers wearing knowing smiles—or were they snickering grins? Before I had time to chicken out, a large man introduced himself as Ernie. He said that Truck 113 should be along any minute and that I should park my car in the lot "over there." He would drive me to the top, where we would wait for the truck.

He asked me if I'd ever seen what comes out of a garbage truck. Handing me a hard hat and a pair of cloth gloves off the pickup truck seat, he explained that rubber gloves weren't safe for picking through all the broken and sharp-edged stuff in the trash. He spoke to me gently. Although he didn't sound really positive, he did give me an ounce of hope that this endeavor might prove fruitful.

As we bounced along in Ernie's truck, I said I hoped I could actually "do this"—meaning deal with the odor and grossness of it all. Ernie quietly reminded me that many people worked here all day; this was their labor. I'm sure I had insulted this large, gentle man; his simple, humble response struck home. A pie of mincemeat proportions splattered on my face. What I deserved was a cow pie; God, thank God, never gives us what we deserve.

When Ernie and I arrived at the top of the heap, I couldn't believe my eyes. The view was spectacular, encompassing several small lakes. The entire area is part of a recreational project, and the huge garbage mound will one day be the site of picnics and toboggan rides. Load by load, the refuse will be covered with earth until suddenly, tons of garbage are transformed into beauty. There is another such former dump the opposite direction from my house, and it is quite lovely.

Ernie chatted with me until Truck 113 arrived, its driver looking like anything but a happy camper. For the first time it occurred to me how self-absorbed my quest had become, how many people's routines were being disrupted.

God's message about pride and arrogance and humility was not escaping me. Here I stood at the top of a mound of garbage becoming totally humbled. My mind unhappily reviewed my haughty pride, my selfishness, my low-life attitude about another man's job. But what was most humbling was not my awareness of all the sinful behavior I had exhibited; it was God's grace. His unrelenting, undeserved love for me.

It was his gentle voice that came out of Ernie's mouth. It was his panoramic fields and lakes that spread before me—ready to cover garbage with grace. It was my hope, God's gift to me, that even I, wretch that I am, could be used to glorify God, just like the trash that was so methodically being transformed.

Stepping down from this mountaintop experience for a moment, however, let me say this: I will spare you the description of what does come out of a dump truck. Let's just say that a brown sort of slime seems to ooze through it all. At least through this load.

Little by little the truck emptied its bowels before me. Ernie called over the driver of a giant piece of earth-moving equipment to occasionally shuffle some of the load from one spot to another so that I could take a fresh look; that should give you some idea as to the enormity of this project. Ernie helped me spot white bags, the weakest and first to rip. Many were nothing more than squashed white clumps of plastic, totally void of their contents. But Ernie kept encouraging my quest. In fact, he wouldn't abandon it until I finally cried wolf.

As we climbed into Ernie's truck for the ride back down the hill, I felt comforted by the fact that at least I had tried. But I was also raging with guilt at the amount of time and equipment I had tied up over airline tickets. I commented on the size of that monster mover and how complicated it must be to operate. Ernie gave me figures on how much per hour that thing costs to operate, and I almost fainted dead away, oozed out of the truck and left myself for live burial. (I quickly thought better of this.)

"Well, the tickets are replaceable," I mumbled, fighting back tears. "It wasn't like I lost a child or anything." And the stinging thankful truth of those words made me lose the battle with my tears.

"Well, it's good you put things in perspective," Ernie said. "Some people just never do." Kind and gentle Ernie.

He told me about the miracle that had transpired once when a lady did actually find an heirloom wedding band. I cried all the more; my pursuit was for paper. Paper easily replaced with money.

But I cried mostly because God loved me anyway. God loved me. I recalled the Scripture that says God's kindness leads us toward repentance (Rom 2:4). Like the garbage hill, I was covered with grace.

All the way home I kept thinking about the lessons I had learned. The graciousness of all those people I hoped I would remember to emulate when the occasion arose—and I knew it would time and time again. I prayed for less of me and more of Christ; I had been witness to power in humble people, God's miraculous power to infiltrate and overcome my pride. I prayed I would remember these lessons the next time someone around me made a mistake. Especially George, who is easy to blame because he's near at hand.

I decided I would have to tell the truth to George. George, who had no idea his wife had been crawling around at the dump all morning. Learning many lessons. Becoming a laughingstock. Becoming transformed in some small way by the love of God. At the top of the garbage.

Unbelievably, quite by accident I found the tickets that same day. I must admit that the discovery did not make me leap with elation; instead, I was totally annoyed that my worry and my dump expedition had been for naught. Until, of course, I realized that the experience was total gain.

I found the tickets in a spot I have no recollection of putting them, but it was definitely I who put them there. They were right behind the bills in my wicker doodah in the cabinet, and I am the only person who ever puts anything there. This was the final humbling twist to this humbling episode, although it was far from the last such experience in my life.

But I knew this without question: God loved me. God loved me enough to orchestrate a trip to the dump that left me humbler and therefore drawn ever closer to him.

"Consider it pure joy, my brothers, whenever you face trials of many kinds, because you know that the testing of your faith develops perseverance" (Jas 1:2). Indeed. Trials produce perseverance. And joy is not an inaccurate name for the fruit of this humbling tale.

Do I wake up every morning and pray for another trial just like it? No way!

Do I take Andrew Murray seriously when he says that humility "must be made the object of special desire, prayer, faith and practice"[3] even if it takes thousands of these episodes? Yes. In Daniel 10:12 a man comes to the prophet in a vision and says, "Do not be afraid, Daniel. Since the first day that you set your mind to gain understanding and to humble yourself before your God, your words were heard, and I have come in response to them."

So I resolve to let each failure turn my heart toward Jesus Christ. Otherwise, I see no joy in humility. It is God who brings the joy. It is our humility that allows his messages to pierce our often pride-filled consciousness. Grace. Unfaltering grace saves us from ourselves.

* * *

The most powerful example of humility is the life, death and resurrection of Christ Jesus himself. In Philippians 2:5-8 Paul tells us that our "attitude should be the same as that of Christ Jesus: Who, being in very nature God, did not consider equality with God something to be grasped, but made himself nothing, taking the very nature of a servant, being made in human likeness. And being found in appearance as a man, he humbled himself and became obedient to death—even death on a cross!"

Christ prayed to God that all of us might be one. "Just as you are in me and I am in you," he said to his Father. "May they also be in us so that the world may believe that you have sent me. I have given them the glory that you gave me, that they may be one as we are one: I in them and you in me. May they be brought to complete unity to let the world know that you sent me and have loved them even as you have loved me" (Jn 17:21-23).

This is the petition of Christ, who, in total surrender, humility and obedience, died for Char the Star.

If you have never read the Scriptures inserting your own name, I suggest you try it. Read it out loud. Dwell on the promises. This might be one of the most humbling experiences a true seeker of Christ and his kingdom will ever encounter.

"You see, at just the right time, when we were still powerless, Christ died for the ungodly, Charlene Ann Brown Baumbich. Very rarely will anyone die for a righteous woman, though for a good woman someone might possibly dare to die. But God demonstrates his own love for us in this: While Charlene, a.k.a. Char the Star, was still a sinner, Christ died for her" (Rom 5:6-8).

* * *

The great I AM is always there for us, each one of us, at all times. As I type these words, I can look over the top of my computer screen and see Lake Wisconsin. It is mid-January and the lake is frozen. Small waves of snow ripple across the top of the ice. Although a wintry blanket of ice and snow lies over everything, it is remarkable how on this day all four seasons are physically represented.

A few dried and brittle leaves cling to tree branches, trying not to let go. When a winter wind whips one down, it flutters onto the cold, white surface below, then skates to a resting place. Remnants of summer are sprinkled all up and down the bank in the form of fishing boats, hoists and stacked pier sections. The lake is outlined by bluffs and the reaching, sprawling branches of trees. Oddly, rain is dancing on the roof this evening, reminding me that spring is always in the making.

It may be that tomorrow everything will look different. But for now, all four seasons envelop this dwelling. And the Lord God, the great I AM, created them all.

"A reverent heart should be the foundation of hearing God," Charles Stanley writes in *How to Listen to God.* "We should be in awe that we can speak to the God who hung the sun and world on nothing, the God who created all the intricacies of human life.

"We should be humble that this same omnipotent God is quietly willing to listen to us, while simultaneously giving direction to the vastness of the universe. His total, concentrated and undisturbed attention is focused upon us individually. That ought to humble us and create within us a reverence that acknowledges God for the mighty Creator He is."[4]

* * *

Incentives for humility? Take your pick. They range from scary to quiet to grandiose to unbelievable. As for my personal favorite, however, it is that humbly dying to self will move me aside and allow God to gloriously live through me.

Bob George, in his book *Classic Christianity,* helps clarify the issue.

As long as I associated the Spirit's ministry only with power, the emphasis was still on me. My prayers were most often, "God, help me to do this activity." God may have been providing some help, but I was still doing it. When I was doing it, there was no lasting joy or fulfillment, and eventually I reached a state of total burnout. Finally I learned that Christ did not come to "help" me serve God; *He came to live His life through me!* I am convinced that many Christians are frustrated with their own spiritual lives because of this same subtle error. This is why Paul wrote: "I have been crucified with Christ and I no longer live, but *Christ lives in me.* The life I live in the body, I live by faith in the Son of God, who loved me and gave Himself for me" (Galatians 2:20).[5]

Bingo! I need not do anything, only humbly get out of the way so Christ can work through me. Can you beat that? Only God can do God's job!

So why do we keep trying, time and time again, only to get caught in the snare of self?

4

Awakenings

Romans 12:2 says we are to be transformed by the renewing of our minds. Truly, the journey from pride to humbleness requires transformation. A transformation that begins with the awakening need for change.

No doubt my time at the dump was a transforming experience. Anytime we truly get a cold, hard look at our selfish selves, a window of opportunity opens. Humbling moments always present occasion for change/transformation.

We need to accept the opportunity, however, and allow God to use it in our lives. Fighting or denying such change keeps us separated from joy. Bucking at God—making excuses, covering our crimes—with our strong-willed selves doesn't bring us freedom; it handcuffs us to our own bucking, thrashing selves.

I know; I've gained many a giant bruise to my ego for even trying! Sometimes the Lord has had to let me thrash around a good long while. When I finally do yield to his will for me, I always wonder what took me so long to let go.

Yes, sometimes transformation begins with a look at ourselves. Other times an awakening begins when we are forced to look outward, to our greater purpose in life.

* * *

It is hard for me to believe that I spent three weeks living in a La-Z-Boy Recliner and three more weeks roosting there, but I am rudely reminded of that life-altering, pathetic fact every time my leg tells me it's going to rain before the TV forecast does.

"You know, Mom," my then eighteen-year-old genius son casually said to me about four years ago as I lay helpless in that La-Z-Boy, "you would have healed a lot faster if you'd done this when you were younger."

He can thank his lucky stars my response was limited to groaning.

In hindsight I can see how much humbler and wiser I became through the experience (and I'll recap those pearls of wisdom for you later), but basically the whole thing was a tribulation from the moment I awoke Friday, March 10, 1989.

FACT: Fairly nice day. Sun shining. Temperatures warming. Snow melting. Layer after layer of dog poop surfacing like land mines.

FACT: Cleaning up dog poop is my job. (I'm the only one who doesn't gag. Farm stock.)

FACT: It won't go away if I ignore it.

As I headed directly for the back yard with tools of the trade and with Butch in tow (I want him to appreciate all I do for him), he presented me with one more evidence of my duties.

About midway through the job, I heard the phone ringing. Not being one to miss an opportunity to do lunch, and wanting to beat my answering machine, I sprinted for the phone, leaving Butch leashed to the spigot on the porch.

No, I didn't fall in a doggie-doo land mine. I did go down, however, making a ninety-degree turn just inside the back door in our kitchen. Crash! Left foot turned under body, right kneecap bashed into steel edge of water cooler.

As I writhed on the floor and screamed at the universe, I heard my perky voice in the background announcing, "I'm sorry, we're unable to come to the phone right now. If you leave a message at the sound of the tone, we'll call you back as soon as we can. Thank you."

No one left a message. And I was in serious trouble. I grabbed my left leg and cried and hollered, then I focused on my right knee and bellowed. Then I broke out in a cold sweat and thought for a moment it was gonna be lights out. No such luck.

After thrashing around on the floor for an indeterminate amount of time, I finally decided I would get up and walk it off. You know, like a stubbed toe. "Get back on that horse," I heard my dad saying after I'd been thrown on my butt. "Shake it off!"

Somehow I managed to hurt, cry, hop and scoot my way from the floor in the kitchen to the La-Z-Boy in the living room—a very long way from the telephone. I soon discovered that the leg above my left ankle looked as if it had sprouted a large gourd, while my right kneecap was already turning shades of awful.

"Don't panic," I said aloud. "You can handle this. You have to." Butch yipped from the porch.

Although I'd never had a broken bone in my forty-three-year-old life, I was ninety-nine percent sure of this one. My kneecap situation wasn't as clear, but the broken leg was becoming more obvious by the moment.

FACT: I needed to get to the phone.

FACT: It hurt like Hades getting there.

FACT: No one in my neighborhood was home except one person who spent five minutes telling me about her double pneumonia. I took a pass on 'fessing up about my leg. Pride doesn't need help that bad.

I phoned the orthopedic doctor, who was gone for the day; his assistant advised me to get to the hospital in Glendale Heights, where their team was on call. She also suggested I notify the hospital of my impending arrival. The hospital receptionist, in turn, advised me to call the paramedics if I was so sure my leg was broken.

No way! I had a broken leg, not a coronary attack or an identity crisis. Char the Star was down but not near death! I decided to get my son, Brian the Genius, out of class from Glenbard West High School.

"Please tell my son he needs to come home," I told the office. "I think I broke my leg. Tell him don't panic; it's not a life-or-death emergency."

Within minutes I heard a terrible screeching of tires. Duke of Hazzard to the rescue!

I'll spare you the details of the torturous loading process (no ambulance for me!) and cut to the bottom line: I went to the hospital in the bed of his 4x4 Toyota pickup. And yes, my leg was broken: a three-inch spiral break of the fibula and another wishbone break off that one. Knee: badly bruised, traumatized and painful, but probably okay.

When my husband arrived at the casting scene—Brian had to get to his after-school job—he thought he'd lighten things up a bit. "I bet she milks this for all it's worth," he said jovially to the attendants. Not funny, George. I made a mental note to prove him right.

By the time we arrived home—to the La-Z-Boy—I had already discovered several of those pearls of humility and wisdom I spoke of earlier. (1) Broken bones hurt real bad, don't try and pretend they don't. Only pride lies to itself and everyone else to cover the truth of pain. (2) If you've ever been sorry you've gained thirty pounds it's when you have to lug it around on crutches. (3) Crutches are awkward and take patience and skill, don't try and act like they don't. (4) I should have changed out of my slacks before I went to the hospital, because they had to cut them—my only slacks that fit—to put on the cast, lest I come home in my underwear—which Mom had always warned me should be clean in case something like this should happen.

Everything I did, including rearranging myself in the La-Z-Boy, caused intense pain—to both legs. I felt stupid. Every little endeavor became a humbling, exhausting adventure.

The pain pills made me gaga. I vowed never to take another. Between a split-level house, a back already suffering from chronic sciatica and the fact that I am a totally impatient person, my personality took a turn toward monstrous and quickly settled there.

It took me only until Saturday morning to realize that lathering everything up when sponge bathing is much easier than figuring out how to rinse. This discovery ranked right up there with the observation that a family enjoys—truly enjoys—having to serve one of its own for about twenty minutes. Especially when she bellows constantly.

The weekend was spent discovering that camping in the La-Z-Boy was easier than trying to maneuver stairs, negotiate "my side" of the bed and sit at the table. I was instructed to rest my foot above my heart as often as necessary to keep the swelling down, which turned out to be a constant need. I was at the mercy of others. Not a familiar place for this in-charge lady.

Little by little, mountains of stuff grew around my La-Z-Boy. The pump-a-drink. Magazines and books to entertain me. Blank paper for thoughts. Remote control and *TV Guide*. Files from work projects. Cordless phone. Hand cream. Ice bag. Towels to hold ice bag in place. Fruit to keep bowels moving under stress. Pens and pencils. Phone books. Purse. Pillows to prop up various body parts. Blankets for bedtime and chills. Aspirin. Miscellaneous tables to hold all the stuff. More stuff.

By Monday, when I was going to be alone for the first time since The Fall, at least until noon when Brian would come home from school to check on me and take Butch out, it seemed as though the bases were covered. Except for the bathroom, which would simply have to be negotiated.

FACT: It's hard to lower oneself onto the toilet while trying to use a knee that hurts because putting the leg with the cast on the ground causes more pain than using the knee that hurts. You start to reconsider the wisdom of having a pump-a-drink so close at hand.

FACT: No matter how many items you're surrounded with, you always need one more.

FACT: You feel insulted when you find out you could have had a choice of colors for your cast, but since you're old, everyone just assumed you wanted white, which you probably would have picked anyway.

BONUS FACT: It's more glamorous to break a bone while skiing than while picking up dog poop.

By Wednesday, I had reached an all-time low. I forgot to have my loved ones bring me my morning tea before they left, so I set out on a quest. After much gnashing of teeth, I finally managed to fill the kettle and get it on the stove, reach the all-too-high-with-a-cast-on shelf where the tea bags rested, and get a spoon and sweetener. As the tea steeped on the counter and I leaned against a chair in exhaustion, I realized there was no way I could get my broken body *and* the cup of tea back to the La-Z-Boy; crutches take two hands and concentration.

A cry-a-thon swept over me that lasted . . . I'd guess in the vicinity of eleven days. The crying basically ceased only for guests, who were very sparse (more reason to cry), and the time it took me to eat the candy most of them brought.

It took three weeks before I could get around with any kind of flow. After every "good" day, it seemed I paid with two bad days for having overdone it. The La-Z-Boy was the only place I could really be comfortable. Imagine: a giant, brown security blanket I could barely stand to live without.

Swelling, insecurity, pain, fear of falling again . . . I started getting real sick of me. When I did manage to get out of the house, the topic of conversation was always, "What happened to you?" "How long do you have to have that thing on?" "Did you break it skiing?" My first few ventures out found me almost desperate to get back to my base.

There was no way to satisfy me. If no one came to see me or asked how I was, I was hurt. When everyone showered attention on me, I hated that too.

Eventually, six weeks after The Fall, the big cast was removed and replaced with an air cast I had to wear for three more weeks. Though physically I didn't need to limp any more, my brain still told me I did. I'd catch myself gimping along and say, "Stop that. You don't have to limp," and I wouldn't—until I'd forget and start limping again. I understand this is quite normal, but again, not being in control is *unacceptable territory.*

Of course now I'm healed—from the worst of it anyway. Old broken bones tend to react like arthritis, letting you know about weather changes and busy days, but the older I get, the more things seem to get better after a good dose of my La-Z-Boy.

As for those final pearls of wisdom, they are many.

Number One: Men (at least the men in my house) don't know where anything in the kitchen is, nor do they ever put it back where they got it; but in the long run it really doesn't matter.

Number Two: Only pride says it doesn't need help when it does. Allowing others to serve you is a lesson in humility. I think of Peter balking when Christ knelt down to wash his feet.

Number Three: Saying the words "If there's anything I can do, let me know" doesn't really mean anything. People who just go ahead and do something, anything, are the ones an invalid remembers.

One of my fondest memories is of a woman whom I'd barely known before this but with whom I've since developed a wonderful relationship. When she heard of my broken leg, she arrived bearing gifts: fruit, a little reading material, candy in the form of Gummy Bear Boogers. (I'm not making this up; there really is such a product. They're, well, booger-shaped and good for many laughs if you've got a quirky sense of humor, which we both do.)

You see, she, too, had spent time in a cast. A much longer time than I ever did, and she knew firsthand my pain and frustration and came to share it with me.

"Praise be to the God and Father of our Lord Jesus Christ, the Father of compassion and the God of all comfort, who comforts us in all our troubles, so that we can comfort those in any trouble with the comfort we ourselves have received from God" (2 Cor 1:3-4).

She even taught me some really cool tricks with the crutches that made the trial much easier to bear.

Number Four, and the most profound lesson, was this: We are blessed when we are able to serve. This ability had to be taken away from me before I ever truly realized that it was a blessing.

"The greatest among you will be your servant. For whoever exalts himself will be humbled, and whoever humbles himself will be exalted" (Mt 23:11-12). Jesus invites us to serve.

Before I could come to any of these conclusions, however, I had to walk through anger. Anger that this had happened to me. I had to put away the tape that said "Get back on that horse" and play a new tape: one that encouraged me to accept where I was. I also could have spared myself bouts of loneliness if, when people called to see if there was anything they could do, I had said, "Yes! Feed my family a meal. Get the dry cleaning. Sit with me; I'm fighting despair and need a friend." Again, pride proved exhausting and defeating. Humbly accepting my lot for the moment would have brought me into the place of rest. Oh, the wisdom of hindsight!

* * *

Servanthood: the ultimate expression of God, perhaps. Through our service, maybe others will see God.

A man came to Mother Teresa after watching one of the Sisters of Mercy care for a patient; the sister had no idea anyone was paying attention. "Mother," the man said to Mother Teresa, "I came here godless. Today I found God in that sister—the way she was looking at the sick person and taking care of him."

"This," Mother Teresa writes, "is what we have been created for—to proclaim Christ's love, to proclaim his presence."[1]

The ability to serve had to be taken away from me before I could appreciate the gift that it is, the blessings that it brings, not only to others but also to me.

Pride doesn't care about humbly serving; it wants to control or to receive a pat on the back for the service. It is fed by external success and thrives on attention. When we get caught up in pride, we can actually exhaust ourselves. Relying on self is always exhausting and risky. Mary Ellen Ashcroft writes in her book *Temptations Women Face,* "No matter what the external success, it never satisfies. . . . If we don't realize this, we will try to control our family and our world; we will feel that we are the ones who have to make everything work." [2]

What a terrible burden we strap ourselves with when we operate out of pride. No one can do it all, and those around us will drop the ball; we all do. We cannot control everything.

When our self-esteem comes from without (works) or, as Ashcroft so correctly calls it, "external success," I do believe it is in conflict with humility. When we think we've done it all—bought airline tickets, helped a friend through a crisis, kept a spotless house (although I'm totally unfamiliar with this), pulled off a near-miraculous fund raiser, won a press award—without giving the honor and glory to Christ who is working through us, then our attitude is the opposite of humility; it is raging pride.

But when our view of self is the knowledge, without a shadow of a doubt, that "we are God's workmanship created in Christ Jesus to do good works, which God prepared in advance for us to do" (Eph 2:10), and that we are his children whom he died to justify, then I believe we can feel not only good but even grand and glorious about ourselves and our purpose—because our glory is in him.

I wish I could remember that before God has to sling pies at me to get my attention. Unfortunately, I sometimes even manage to wear several dripping messes at a time.

* * *

You'd think my broken-leg experience would have taught me, once and for all, the servant message. Wrong! Not long afterward I nearly forgot all about the joy of serving—even when I got paid for it.

I had accepted a health-care magazine's assignment to write about a wonderful, dedicated woman who headed up a hospital. Although the publication didn't pay much, I felt obligated, as always, to do my best. Then I received the background information on this woman; it arrived in a U-Haul (slight enhancement of fact). Among the many newspaper clippings, biographical information and on and on and on, her public relations person had gone so far as to include a paperback book about the history of the hospital my subject was in charge of.

"If someone thinks I'm supposed to take the time to read all *this* stuff for what I'm getting paid, they're vastly mistaken," I said to no one, as I sat surrounded by endless documents. But then my conscience, that quiet voice within, started getting the best of me. Perhaps there would be something of profound interest in the paperback. Perhaps I should at least skim it. Flip through a couple chapters and skim a few paragraphs. Okay, maybe even read a page here and there. Grudgingly, I began.

About five minutes into this project an unsuspected pie blasted my face. Its impact nearly choked me. This probably wouldn't have happened except for the fact that the pie hit when I had my mouth open—because I was busy grumbling.

Seems that back in history, this hospital went through a near-desperate financial crisis. When things were looking the bleakest, the office received an anonymous gift of twenty-five thousand dollars. This was back when twenty-five thousand dollars actually did something. The timing couldn't have been better.

When I first began reading about the gift, I suspected it had come from somebody who had inherited a lot of money, or perhaps a person whose life had been saved by the care given in the hospital. No, maybe a close relative of the donor had died at the hospital, and the bereft donor wanted a wing named in that person's honor. When I came upon the actual reason, however, the spring-loaded pie sailed into my face.

The note that came with the check explained that the donor was grateful. He was grateful for the opportunity to have had a job selling newspapers at that hospital when he was twelve years old. That job had helped his family survive during the Depression, and he had never forgotten it. He had vowed to himself to pay them back one day if he could, and so he did.

Here I sat in my comfy home office, wearing comfy clothes, able to drink tea out of my favorite mug while I worked. Research materials had been delivered to my door via the United States Postal System. Travel expenses downtown for the interview would be reimbursed. I was getting paid to learn about a woman who, it turned out, greatly inspired me. (A perennial perk of journalism: the opportunity to find out firsthand what makes people tick. What made this lady tick was God!) And I was complaining.

This holy pie brought repentance and thanksgiving—for the opportunity to work. It can best be described as a humble pie. I wish I could be sure I'll never have to eat another; in fact, though, I'm sure I will.

* * *

Awakenings don't always come through shame-filled moments; sometimes they come through an outpouring of God's blessings. A bountiful, overwhelming shower of goodness, and we can find no explanation for why it has come our way.

Several years ago my friend Mary Beth and I decided we would try writing a novel together. We seemed to share a humorous, somewhat quirky view of motherhood and "wifedom." Once a week for a year and a half, we met and edited the previous week's work that we'd done separately. Throughout this year, our lives took many twists and turns: George dealt with a bout of unemployment; Mary Beth became pregnant and had a miscarriage; I suffered through a major midlife crisis; Mary Beth became pregnant and delivered a son. George landed full-time employment. And one day, our book was finished.

We knew this: No matter what else, we wanted to become published authors. We were writers—in fact, we decided we were pretty darn good writers. But we hadn't yet been published.

After our project was completed, and just about the time we began seriously to try marketing the manuscript, life, as it has a way of doing, took us on very different courses: I was given opportunities to write for newspapers and magazines as well as an invitation to author a nonfiction book; Mary Beth's middle child was diagnosed with cancer. Our joint fiction project was quickly put aside.

I was filled with excitement the day I opened my mailbox and found a letter from a publisher asking whether I was

interested in writing books. Yet my very core was being consumed with guilt.

"Why me, God? Why me?" This question is usually asked
in times of trial; my searching came from life-altering goodness. My guilt feelings nearly shut me down for a while. What
had I done to deserve my heart's desire? I knew what a wretch
I was. How had I fooled all these people? Why am I signing
a contract and Mary Beth, who is a wonderful writer and
mother with a sweet spirit who wants to be published as much
as I do, is finding herself holding a daughter who is retching
from chemotherapy, making crazed, scary drives in the middle of the night to the emergency room while trying to figure
out what to do with her two other little children . . . "Why,
God? Why?"

I went into a local Christian bookstore and said, "I know
you have a book called *When Bad Things Happen to Good
People.* Do you perhaps have one titled *When Good Things
Happen to Bad People?"*

Now don't misunderstand. I have never considered myself
hopeless; I cling to God's promises; I know his love. But this
had really thrown me for a spiritual loop.

And then one day the awakening hit me: Did I think Mary
Beth and her precious young daughter deserved what they
and the rest of their family were getting? Of course not! Then
how could I think I did, or did not, deserve what was dealt
to me for the moment? I had become so distraught with guilt
that I was, in fact, hardly remembering to be thankful for my
bounty—and this had plunged me into further despair that
I could be so thankless!

All this in response to goodness.

Slowly I came to understand that none of us get what we deserve, praise God! Oh, it's not that I didn't already believe that somewhere in the recesses of my heart, but now it had been crystallized. It was God who had opened all those doors for publication. He had a message; he had a plan; I was to be his vessel. It simply had nothing to do with whether anything was deserved or not—good or bad.

When I was finally able to be honest with Mary Beth about this struggle, she delivered the most humbling of gifts hidden in this awakening, and gently opened my eyes to God's omniscient love. Mary Beth did not ponder the injustice of the situation. What Mary Beth spoke to me about was how good God had been to her throughout all of her trials, especially her daughter's cancer. God was good, she said. She was so grateful. She was so thankful for his love.

* * *

Here at the lake, yesterday's pattering rain has changed to today's furiously blowing flakes. The opposite bank is shrouded in white haze; I can't see the two small islands off to the right, but I know they are there. Although I am pleasantly warm—legs wrapped in a wool and flannel blanket, heat vent at my feet—cool air seeps through the bank of windows and encircles my fingers as they tap on the keyboard. Yesterday I speculated that things might be totally different today; indeed they are, but not because spring has arrived.

The sound of wind blowing through the trees brings to mind John 3:8: "The wind blows wherever it pleases. You hear its sound, but you cannot tell where it comes from or where it is going. So it is with everyone born of the Spirit."

It occurs to me, then, that our job is to be ready to move, in whatever direction God would have us, at the sound of his whisper and with total confidence. Preferably without questions, though he always listens to our questions anyway. Sorting everything out is not our job. "Trust in the LORD with all your heart and lean not on your own understanding; in all your ways acknowledge him, and he will make your paths straight" (Prov 3:5).

After all my fretting about who did or didn't deserve what, I realized that only pride would even try to figure it all out; humility would simply accept. Not that the Bible isn't full of examples of people who cried out to the Lord. If we are torn by painful questions and a deep sense of injustice, God knows it anyway, even if we hold it all inside. But only humility allows God to heal our wounds; pride is closed to his warm hands. Pride wants to own it all: good, bad and dubious.

Recently I bought a T-shirt decorated with a black-and-white stick drawing of quirky, grinning angels. The shirt reads, "Angels can fly because they take themselves lightly." Now there's an awakening: get rid of the extra baggage or you'll weigh yourself down with it. Airborne. What a thought!

Again, a gust of wind rattles the windows. I find I cannot stop thinking about wind, Spirit, flight, trust. I remember the first time I went up in a hot-air balloon. It was a heavenly experience, unlike anything I had imagined.

I had imagined hearing the whoosh of wind streaming by as the balloon swept through the sky. Not so. The balloon moves in the stream of the wind. You are the wind, so to speak. It is perfectly quiet in the basket of the hot-air balloon, except for the occasional blasts of the burners and the sounds that echo up from earth.

The balloon rider cannot chart a definite course; different elevations capture different currents. Sure, you can go up and down and try and hitch a ride on one of the many currents, but basically you are at the mercy of the wind, and it doesn't always blow in the direction or at the speed you'd planned— which means that balloon riders land in some interesting places and positions. Like in someone's back yard or your face.

God's Spirit blows and we "cannot tell where it comes from or where it is going." But we can trust him; he always knows what he's doing. We need only hop on for the ride, listen and yield. Stay light enough to fly with him.

Balloons are constructed by human beings. The basket that you stand in and the tank and burner that fill the envelope (balloon part) with hot air are engineered and manufactured by people. And people then entrust their well-being to things that they themselves have created, hoping that the balloon is engineered well enough to keep them from crashing down to earth.

Don't mistake my message: I would go up in a hot-air balloon again without hesitation. In fact, I have. But let's use the balloon as a metaphor for human pride. Would you rather travel in the balloon or with the Spirit—for the rest of your life and through some terrible storms? Whose creation would you rather trust: God's or your own?

Of course God lands us in some pretty unexpected places too. And sometimes it's flat on our face should we insist on our own way.

* * *

"I will instruct you and teach you in the way you should go; I will counsel you and watch over you. Do not be like the horse or the mule, which have no understanding but must be controlled by bit and bridle or they will not come to you" (Ps 32:8-9).

Trust me, you don't want to have to be coerced. I was raised around horses, and it was sometimes quite painful to watch the tactics that had to be used on a horse that refused to stand still for a vet or load into a trailer. Bit and bridle are tame instruments; for horses that were particularly un-cooperative there was a device called a twitch that is even worse than it sounds. It is a wooden handle with a loop of rope secured to the end. The loop is wrapped around the horse's upper lip, then twisted. This experience is worse than plucking twenty nose hairs at once. I'll take a holy pie any day, thank you very much!

Keep in mind that bits and bridles and twitches are not used as means of punishment. Animal caretakers sometimes must resort to them in order to properly minister to an un-cooperative animal. Sadly enough, the twitch would some-times have to be used to get a horse into a trailer so that it could be taken to a lovely green retirement pasture. We had to put a twitch on a horse to get it to its resting place. Sound vaguely familiar?

Thank goodness Christ came to us as a gentle shepherd. "He is patient with you, not wanting anyone to perish, but everyone to come to repentance" (2 Pet 3:9).

* * *

There is another kind of awakening that I must talk about. It is the kind of awakening that happens when you realize that in your own power you are absolutely incapable to make something happen. You are at the end of you. You have no power or earthly means of changing what needs to be changed. And then comes the pie.

Let me tell you a story.

This is a story about bad behavior, at least in my opinion. Others might refer to it as doing what's natural, blowing off steam, getting out your frustrations, losing control, responding in a healthy manner, expressing yourself . . . but I believe it's flat-out bad behavior.

I am talking about temper displayed on the golf course, and this is a subject with which I am intimately acquainted. Even though because of my back injury it's been many years since I've trekked a course, simply recalling these moments tightens my shoulders and knots my stomach. Ah, the memories. Sand stuck on my lip gloss—caked, to be exact, after three shots in the same trap. No-brain putting. Runs of excessive bad luck, like discovering someone had just played *my ball on my best shot of the day*. Repeated trips over the same green.

Although I do not remember actually hurling any clubs, at least with an excessive amount of force, I certainly did my share of dropping the club, raising my hands in the air in an exaggerated shrug, then picking the club up and spearing it into my golf bag. I then (1) stood staring into space while trying to calm down as I recited internal parental messages, or (2) grabbed my cart's handle and stalked twenty feet to my left where the ball was lying, or (3) moved ten feet to the right if I had toed it, or (4)—probably the worst scenario—didn't have to move at all for my next shot.

I have become mute. I have thrown a hissy fit after holing a ball from twenty yards off the green—for a 13. (Three visits to the same creek running along the fairway.) I have quit after five holes. I have given up and finally aimed for the lake. I have always been embarrassed at my behavior, yet I seemed incapable of changing it. (If there was golf back in biblical times, perhaps this was the thorn in Paul's flesh.)

What is it about the sport that brings out the worst in me and many others I know? Was golf invented by Satan, do you suppose?

"It is the most frustrating sport I have ever played," Bob said. (All names except those of assistant pros have been changed; otherwise, some of them might never get a golf date.)

"Everyone thinks they could be better and should be better," said Brett, assistant pro at a local club.

Except my husband.

"I am golfing good for my capabilities," said George (husband's real name). He is content with his rounds because he knows he doesn't golf enough to live up to his potential.

An explosive friend of mine takes a different approach—one that I can relate to. "The only thing that makes it worthwhile is the competition," Fred said. "Even if I am only competing against myself."

Against myself. Interesting. Pressure's on, immediately setting up a space in which to fall short.

Having to deal with other people's tempers is what gets to Hal. He recently told me about a time he was golfing at Medinah Country Club with a guy who three times threw his club into the woods along a fairway, then ordered his caddie to fetch it.

After the third episode, Hal waved the pooped caddie over to him and put the man's club in his own bag. The next time the guy looked for his club, Hal announced, "You threw it away three times. It doesn't belong to you anymore."

But let's return to the main thrust: most people get mad at themselves. "Some are more demonstrative than others," Brett said. This is why clubs end up in lakes, broken over knees and in trees.

"A friend of mine threw his entire bag up into a tree," Brett said. "He had to climb up and get it out."

"Did he learn anything from that experience?" I asked.

"I think he got a little better," he replied. Temperwise, at least.

"I've learned to control my temper, I guess," said Chuck, another assistant pro. "It's not worth it, and it costs too much money." Especially if you are prone to breaking and bending things. And I don't imagine you'd last very long at the "pro" level with the reputation of a maniac. Although just last week I heard Jack Nicklaus admit on television that he had broken many clubs. Never on camera, of course.

The main reason anger on the golf course is not worth it, however, is one everyone agrees on, and it's more universal than golf: if you can't let go of the anger, it makes your game even worse. And your life. Not only that, if everyone took Scripture's advice to heart, perhaps the courses would be empty. "Do not make friends with a hot-tempered man, do not associate with one easily angered, or you may learn his ways and get yourself ensnared" (Prov 22:24-25). And Proverbs 29:11 says, "A fool gives full vent to his anger, but a wise man keeps himself under control."

"Everybody gets mad," Ken said. "It's how they handle it that matters." Ken turns his back on bad shots—other people's bad shots, that is. Other people who have temper tantrums, to be exact.

"I do a lot of looking off in the distance so I don't laugh," he said. "They are acting like children; and if they could see themselves, they would laugh too. But you better not laugh, because you won't be their friend very long." I would like to take a moment to thank Ken, a friend of mine, for his restraint and commendable behavior when in my foursomes.

One day God, through his holy grace, served unsuspecting me a hefty dose of humbling perspective on the fairway through a stranger I had been teamed up with. About the third hole on one of my worst rounds ever, I started complaining—to put it mildly—about my game, and how I was fighting to control an outburst so as not to embarrass myself and ruin this chap's day.

"Honey," he said, "I've had four heart attacks, and I'm just thankful to be out here hitting a bad shot."

Whish! Splat!

I would say this holy pie was of the apple variety. Chunks of it slid down my face and coated me throughout the rest of the round and all the way to the clubhouse when it was over. Henceforth I shall continue to pick chunks off myself every time I allow needless anger to rise in me. All the while, of course, I am licking the sweet truth of these chunks off my lips. Isn't God good?

"I thank my God every time I remember you" (Phil 1:3), Mr. Angel on the golf course who delivered a holy pie, up close and personal and with great wisdom. Mr. Angel, who wielded gentleness rather than a twitch.

* * *

Awakenings. God's Spirit calling us to ride the wind, to trust his control, to enter the freedom of humility. Nudges and whispers, invitations.

Lord, keep pricking my heart into wakefulness.

5

The
Power
Within

OW does humility happen?

" 'Not by might nor by power, but by my Spirit,' says the
LORD Almighty" (Zech 4:6). And Andrew Murray explains,

No outward instruction, not even of Christ Himself—no
argument, however convincing; no sense of the beauty of
humility, however deep; no personal resolve or effort,
however sincere and earnest—can cast out the devil of
pride.

It is only by the indwelling of Christ in His divine humility that we become truly humble.[1]

The story I'm about to tell could not have been resolved without Christ's power within. It happened not long ago.

* * *

After a lengthy period of simmering anger—will I never learn, even after I've stockpiled shelves and shelves of holy apple pie filling?—I realized that my rage was debilitating me. If I was to keep functioning at the pace I needed to in order to meet my commitments, I had to forgive someone. Even though the offending person would never know I'd forgiven him—because I had never revealed my anger to him—it was necessary for my own mental health and spiritual survival.

It's my experience that festering anger clouds truth and hardens hearts. Open wounds ooze and run and infect everything they come in contact with. Just like scratching chicken pox.

The anger and hurt were exhausting and consuming me. Try as I might to reconcile myself to this person's ongoing behavior, I could not. The more I scratched, the more the infection spread. One day in conversation with a friend, something I said showed me that my inwardly bubbling anger toward the offender was beginning to leak. Soon afterward it struck me like a bolt of lightning that if I truly wanted to be healed from this anger and get on with my life before I consumed myself altogether, I needed to forgive. But try as I might to do that, I could not.

Finally, in near exhaustion, I arrived at the end of my self-efforts. I prayed to God for a miracle. I prayed that my heart would change before it cracked from its own brittleness. I asked God to open me to his unconditional love and allow it to flow through me. It was an absolutely sincere request, inspired by desperation. I did it for me, not for the person who had wounded me. I cried and surrendered. I did not expect anything to happen, but I gave God my will.

Unfortunately, it seems that all too often it's only in exhaustion that this solution of surrender occurs to me. Fortunately, each time I do it, it gets a little easier.

The next morning I awoke with wild thoughts that could not have sprung from my own goodness; I had none at that point. The miracle was this: I felt mercy for the person I needed to forgive. I could hardly believe my own thoughts, but they were sincere. I realized for the first time that I had no idea what I might be like if I had walked in his shoes. I became aware that perhaps his behavior was rooted in past suffering, in his need to survive difficult circumstances when he was growing up. His home life had been a far cry from the loving, stable environment I was reared in.

I hurt for him. I could not believe it, but I truly did. I hurt for him so badly that I wept again—this time for him, not myself. My hardened heart was softened; thankfulness leaped from my lips.

"Dear Lord, you have worked another miracle in my life. You have moved a mountain. You have given me the gift of mercy." I thanked God for all that was good in my life as a child, and mourned for what the person I had forgiven had missed. I prayed that the Lord would comfort him during the difficult time we were both walking through. I asked God to help me minister to him as well, that I might be used as an expression of God's love. I actually desired all this. Unbelievable.

When I saw him later that day, I had an inexplicable urge to wrap my arms around him, and I did. He never knew what all had transpired in my heart. Although I still believe his behavior was hurtful to many people, to say the least, Christ and his unconditional love through the power of his indwelling Holy Spirit fashioned a change in me—a change that I could never have mustered up for myself.

Psalm 126 says, "The LORD has done great things for us, and we are filled with joy" (v. 3). The people of Israel were joyful over the restoration of Zion. And I too had been restored. "Those who sow in tears will reap with songs of joy. He who goes out weeping, carrying seed to sow, will return with songs of joy, carrying sheaves with him" (vv. 5-6).

Once you learn to humbly come before God with your needs, take a leap of faith that he'll meet them, then lay down your will before him (and that is the most difficult part), an unbelievable burden flutters away.

The first step is an act of humility. It takes a lot of guts to put down your will. What might you find if you do? Fear? Vulnerability? Your own shortcomings? "Humility is the courage to dare," says Lloyd John Ogilvie. "Authentic humility is an outward expression of gratitude, honesty and courage."[2]

Although I believe that to be true, I also have to caution myself against believing that my courageous acts *bring about* humility. That would be pure pride. Still, I do know for a fact that letting go of one's will, especially when it's as strong as mine, definitely is an act of courage. It is perhaps the hardest thing I ever do. And it is an act of obedience when, by grace, I can actually do so.

Now I could become my own whipping post and launch into a lengthy diatribe about my shortcomings. But I'm learning that the point is not to remain occupied with myself. That doesn't bring glory to God—regardless of whether I'm thinking about how low or how wonderful I am. Self-absorption is not the answer; it simply entangles me further in pride.

What *is* the answer? Jesus in me.

Paul's prayer for the Ephesian Christians (Eph 3:14-21) nails what I'd like to say here. So I'll just let him say it.

For this reason I kneel before the Father, from whom his whole family in heaven and on earth derives its name. I pray that out of his glorious riches he may strengthen you with power through his Spirit in your inner being, so that Christ may dwell in your hearts through faith. And I pray that you, being rooted and established in love, may have power, together with all the saints, to grasp how wide and long and high and deep is the love of Christ, and to know this love that surpasses knowledge—that you may be filled to the measure of all the fullness of God.

Now to him who is able to do immeasurably more than all we ask or imagine, according to his power that is at work within us, to him be glory in the church and in Christ Jesus throughout all generations, for ever and ever! Amen.

* * *

Funny thing about the indwelling Spirit: he has a way of literally flinging or flipping pies. At least in my friend Marlene's case.

Marlene told me about the time she volunteered to make two quiches (just like pies) for a women's gathering. Now Mar is good at making quiche. In fact, she is good at making just about anything. She is what I would classify as a gourmet cook. She even has copies of *Gourmet* magazine on the bookshelves in her bathroom, and we all know that's where a lot of our most serious reading gets done. If ever I'm in doubt as to what to add to or subtract from a recipe, or what spice I should use to get the desired effect, Mar's the one I call. (I also call her with spelling emergencies, but that's besides the point.) In fact, I phoned her just the other day to ask her if there was any way to compensate for too much salt in a batch of soup. Of course she knew: add chunks of potato. And it worked!

But I fear I have digressed. Let me get back to quiche, which is just like pie, of course.

As Mar prepared the quiches, she tells me, "I became enthralled with how wonderful I was to make these two wonderful quiches. I was bursting with pride." They were beautiful, she claims, and I don't doubt her for a moment. Anyway, she was heading out the door with her wonderful self and her wonderful quiches, and the screen door somehow slammed back on her. It hit the edge of the tray, and the two wonderful quiches fell flat, face down on her entryway floor. "It looked like someone had done a big puke job there," she said, mincing no words. That's my friend Mar!

The still small voice inside her then began making some points about her attitude. "I wasn't making those pies for those people," she admits. "I was thinking how wonderful I was. Now, as soon as I start thinking about and doing something really smashing and it is not for the right purpose, I remember my two quiches."

Like me, Mar found that the telling of one tale of humiliation seems to cause the recollection of another. I was all too happy to listen to someone else's humbling stories for a change.

Not only is Mar a good cook, but she also plays bells in the bell choir at our church. One Sunday, Mar said, the pastor had been praying for someone during the service, and she found herself making a snide comment. Guess what? During the bell choir's rendition of "Crown Him with Many Crowns," Mar, to her total humiliation, played the wrong bell. She believes that something within her made it happen. "I had made fun of someone during prayer," she said.

She admitted her sin to her fellow bell-choir members. She says they pooh-poohed the notion that she rang the wrong bell as a result of her behavior, but she is convinced. "I feel that God was teaching me a lesson."

Now Mar doesn't believe in going around thrashing herself for this; she learned her lesson. As she said, when she gets to feeling a little too wonderful, she remembers the quiche. And John 14:26 tells us that the Holy Spirit will remind us what he has taught us. Our job is to act with obedience once we remember. I have to personally admit, however, to learning some of the same lessons time and time again. In fact, I'm sure you've already caught on to that.

* * *

I feel it would be appropriate to add a cake story here. Even though cake isn't pie, I believe them to be closely related as they are both wonderful. Next to Cheetos they are possibly nature's most perfect foods.

Years ago, I invited my parents over for Mom's birthday. They were going out to dinner with friends, and it seemed natural to extend the invitation for cake to all of them. They happily accepted.

The apartment we lived in had a minuscule kitchen; it was really just a narrow hallway. When I needed to open the oven door, no one could be sitting at the kitchen table. The oven also tended to have an uneven temperature, so the two cake halves came out lopsided. That was okay, three-year-old Bret and I decided, because we could cleverly fit them together and fill in the uneven places with frosting, and so we did. Lots of frosting. And then some more.

We decorated the top of that cake with even more frosting. We wrote greetings on it; we created flowers. When we were finished it was beautiful, and we were excited. So excited, in fact, that we decided it needed to make a dramatic entrance, so we hid it in my bedroom to await the perfect moment.

When the timing was just right, I didn't just get the cake, I heralded its arrival. With much dramatic emphasis, I recounted every last time-consuming detail of its creation—excluding, of course, any mention of its hidden defects.

Much to my horror, when I flipped on the light in the bedroom, what I found was this: the top layer had slid off the bottom layer; the frosting—and all its beautiful flowers and cursive writing—had slid off the top layer, oozing onto the edge of the plate and the top of my dresser.

Although this was, to say the least, terribly disappointing—not to mention a nasty mess—there was a blessing involved, and it came via the sense of humor my parents had spent a lifetime nurturing in me. Laughter brought a wonderfully cleansing moment, and we found that the cake tasted good in spite of its pathetic appearance.

My point is this: what comes out of us is what's bubbling inside, whether it's humor, anger or Spirit-filled love. This moment of potential disaster instead erupted in grace.

Grace—unearned, undeserved kindness—was showered

upon us by my parents and their friends through the gift of laughter. And of course my mom, in her bountiful love, convinced Bret and me that this was her favorite cake among all those that had ever been made for her. And perhaps it was. Mom bubbled inside with love; we received it. Both my parents bubbled with laughter and great passion; we received it and grew our own.

My earthly mother and father planted good things in me, but what God begins, he finishes—for eternity. "For I am confident of this very thing, that He who began a good work in you will perfect it until the day of Christ Jesus" (Phil 1:6 NASB). This is a hope-filled Scripture. I even claimed it for my boys; they were definitely two good works God began in me.

Of course the catch is this: "every project you undertake can be accomplished your way or God's way."[3] And as the title of the old television series "Father Knows Best" says, there's no doubt who ought to be in charge.

* * *

How can we be sure who's running the show, even when our intentions are to allow God control? I wish I had a pat few paragraphs to make it all clear; in fact, that is one of my biggest questions. Doubt swirls around me much of the time, just as it did around Thomas, one of my favorite apostles, who was never afraid to ask questions. (And Christ always gently obliged him with answers.) I believe it's a constant struggle to discern our motives, especially for those of us with strong wills. Especially since fooling ourselves is so easy to do.

"Yes, God wants us to have this new couch. Why wouldn't he? It is the desire of my heart."

"Of course I'm in God's will; I prayed."

"Running away from all this is exactly what God wants me to do. After all, even Scripture tells us we're to pick up our cross and follow him, and I'm sure he's ready to blow this joint! Who wouldn't be?"

Okay, maybe these are questionable examples, but you know what I mean. Self-justification is easy to come by and eases guilt; that's why we love it. At least for a while. And Christians are just as self-deceptive as anyone, perhaps more than others because we're so quick to tout our praying, God-seeking selves.

But the great thing is, that indwelling still small voice always seems to whisper in my ear, even when I don't want it to, causing me to run smack into myself. Maybe the key to letting go and letting God is learning to listen to that inner voice. And then following it, even if it doesn't feel very good. And many times it won't.

In a noise-polluted world, amid a steady stream of free advice, hearing that voice can become tricky. There are always television talk shows and radio broadcasts (including Christian programs) that fill our heads with others' stories and tried-and-true solutions. They influence our thought patterns, even when we're unaware they're doing so. God's will in someone else's life is not necessarily his will for us, but it's easy to buy into. That latest self-help book or magazine article is there to try to convince us to take this or that step.

And there are all those worthless thoughts knocking around in our brains and taking up space.

I recently saw a magazine ad for a gizmo that attaches to your vacuum sweeper and cuts your hair. Somehow you set it for the length you want your hair to be; it draws your hair up the tube, where, apparently, whirring blades whack it off. Can you imagine this in the hands of a toddler? Do-it-yourself disaster! Weed whipper gone berserk! The odd thing is, as useless to me as this idea is, it has taken root in one of my brain cells and has become part of the garbage that bubbles inside me.

How do we silence all the stuff we are bombarded with daily so we can become sensitive to the inner stirrings? Becoming nuns or monks just isn't in the cards for most of us.

"Be still, and know that I am God" (Ps 46:10 NIV). "Cease striving and know that I am God" (NASB). "Let be then; learn that I am God" (REB). "Stand silent! Know that I am God!" (LB).

The Holy Word doesn't say we have to do this twenty-four hours a day, but it does say "Do it!" I don't doubt for a minute that the Great I AM is capable of pushing all else aside, even dumb thoughts like having your hair sucked up into a vacuum, if we give him a quiet chance to do so.

In *Knowing God* J. I. Packer tells us: "What matters supremely, therefore, is not, in the last analysis, the fact that I know God, but the larger fact which underlies it—the fact that He knows me."[4] And when God knows you, he knows you. Thus, returning to the question of motives and control, I'd say the answer seems to be this: Be still and know him; he will reveal you and your motives. He will, without a doubt, let you know who's in control, even if he has to wing pies at you to get your attention.

Thou dost scrutinize my path and my lying down,
And art intimately acquainted with all my ways.

Even before there is a word on my tongue,
Behold, O LORD, Thou dost know it all.
(Ps 139:3-4 NASB)

"Thou dost know it all." There's no fooling God. Know God; know self; know who's got the reins. Be still; cease striving; let be then; stand silent; listen.

Search me, O God, and know my heart;
Try me and know my anxious thoughts;
And see if there be any hurtful way in me,
And lead me in the everlasting way.
(Ps 139:23-24 NASB)

But silence isn't the only way to hear and know God. He often speaks through the people around us—family, friends, strangers. He shines his face on us through them, and shows us what he is like.

Mom and Dad with their laughter over a cake. Ernie and all the others at the garbage dump. The stranger who teamed up with me on a golf course and delivered God's message. Mary Beth as she spoke of God's love in the midst of her crisis. Each was the voice and hands and body of Christ. Loving Char the Star. Each stirring that space inside me where goodness and pure love dwell. Each stirring the Christ within. The power within to transform rubbish into beauty.

All our lives he is shaping us, loving us, calling us, being with us so that he can be at home in us. In all our bright celebrations and deep disappointments, all our shining moments and dark days, all our victories and defeats, he is there. Whispering, calling, shaping, loving. Nothing in our lives, nothing that is our life, is apart from him or ever has been or ever will be. . . .

We have to find some time to be still and see the grace that surrounds us, to be open to the touch of the hand that is leading us. We have to find the time to listen to the voice of a God who whispers.[5]
Peggy Benson, the woman who penned those words, encourages us to listen to our lives. Our lives are memory portfolios, full of stories. We need to pay attention, to heed our memories, to listen to what God is saying through all the events and the people that fill the pages of these stories.

Surely, if I listen to my own stories on the pages of this book, as well as other pages I have written—and not written—I will be in the circle of Know God; Know Self. Surely his unwavering, unconditional love will penetrate me with humbling power through the recollection of his past blessings and faithfulness in my life.

And your life, too, has its own stories to listen to. Lend them your ear.

6

Does
Humility
Show?

WHAT good is talking about humility if we don't
find it in action? Problem is, we've already touched on how
easy it is to function with wrong motives and incentives (my
way or God's way), and there is always the possibility that
what we perceive as a humble act or meek personality could
instead be camouflage for some rotten undergirdings. And
even the most well-intentioned people can act in ways that
don't seem humble at all. Only God Incarnate can be trusted
for a pure example of humility.

Many of the books I've pored through have made the point

that the minute we are aware of a truly humble act of our own, we've lost humility because now we're thinking about us. I've done a lot of pondering over these kinds of statements. Most of the time I believe them to be true; however, I imagine I'll be tossing around some related questions the rest of my life.

I guess if we recognize the moment or act of humility as God's presence in the situation, we're okay; if we think it's us being good, we've lost it. Maybe. Unless when we did it, it was pure. Then it's only after the fact that we've lost it.

What keeps me from being totally persuaded that an aware person cannot be humble is the way one can be washed with light when one has acted not out of self but out of humility, with no ulterior motive or incentive. Now would it be fair to say that the minute I recognized this washing with light, the lights go out? Does it not become a part of us, filling us and bubbling inside us, and nurturing and comforting us as we move forward?

The story about the man who told Mother Teresa he had seen God in the nun seems pertinent here. Remember, Mother Teresa said the nun wasn't aware anyone was watching her. Then again, maybe she had seen the watching man out of the corner of her eye and became full of herself and her good works (like Mar with her quiches) and really laid it on thick for show. Part of me doesn't believe that, however, because the man did see God through the nun's love. There was something more than her in that room. But we shall never know. And if the man saw God *even if* the nun was putting on a show, what does that mean?

Though this chapter is taking up some confusing questions,

I think the issues are important to explore. As you've already noticed, I'm full of questions—more questions than answers. But I do believe this: we need to remember that we can actually know nothing about another's true motives. Only God does. And it is before him that we stand.

* * *

One of my favorite and easiest sources of little tidbits for this chapter has been the Sunday magazine of the *Chicago Tribune.* Near the front of the magazine there is a weekly feature called "Fast Track" with Cheryl Lavin's byline. Rather than an actual write-up about an entertainment-industry person, it's simply a profile based on a questionnaire: occupation, birthday, real name, current home, marital status, children, car, working on . . . , last good movie I saw, three words that best describe me . . . The answers usually don't exceed ten words. We're not talking depth here, but these celebrity profiles are kind of fun to read, especially when you're writing a book about humility and one of the items is "my most humbling experience."

The identities of the celebrities don't matter to me here, just the answers. Sometimes they're very revealing, other times they're flippant. Perhaps if we could hear the tone of voice the answers were given in it would make a difference to our interpretation. Here are a few of these "most humbling experiences":

☐ The 15th-anniversary show of "Saturday Night Live." I stood next to all these comedic heroes of mine. I had wanted to be on the show since I was a boy.

☐ Working with the Special Olympics.

☐ Looking around the locker room in high school.

☐ I can't think of any.

I don't think this last answer was supposed to be funny. I'm not standing in judgment of this person, but I also don't think she's someone I'd want to do lunch with. I doubt we have much in common.

If I had to tell someone my most humbling moment, I'd have a difficult time; there are so many zillions of them to choose from. Yet one jumps into the forefront of my mind at this moment.

As you can imagine, it can be a little tricky to keep your pride under firm control when you're autographing books. In fact, I've decided it's impossible. It's a cliché to say that seeing your book in print is like looking at your newborn baby for the first time, but in a way that's a good parallel. A book *is* something we birth. First there's conception, then growing . . . Anyway, like a new parent, the newly published author generally feels not only awe and wonder but also pride in the creation. Yup. I'd be lying if I said anything else. Although I realize that everything was a gift—the talent, the opportunity, the very children I wrote about—pride still swells whenever I see *Don't Miss Your Kids!* on a bookshelf in a store. And especially one time when I saw it on a rack that said, "What's New, What's Hot!" I was absolutely in pig's heaven.

I couldn't stop thinking about the person who spoke once in a writing class I attended. She said the first time she had a magazine article in print, she went from store to store with her son. She had him run over to the magazine rack, pick up the issue and say, very loudly, "Isn't this the one your article's in?" You gotta love that joy. At least I did. I identified with her exuberance—although I never went quite as far as she. I hope. I'll let you be the judge.

It's a funny thing about having a book out and occasionally being in the public eye: sometimes people act as if they're imposing when they request an autograph. I'm always shocked at this notion; I'm honored that anyone would *want* my autograph. In fact, I'm amazed.

One signing I had at a local Christian bookstore just threw me over the deep end, for a number of reasons. I was at the mall about a week before the signing, and the managers had turned practically the entire store (slight exaggeration, but not totally inaccurate) into The Baumbich Wonderland. The signing was to take place on Mother's Day, and of course they were trying to draw business, but let me tell you, it was really something for Char the Star to see. My book was displayed in no fewer than four areas—and there were lots of copies. A big poster stood on an easel in the entryway. Beside a color photograph of me and a dust jacket, the poster said, "Meet the Author. Receive a free carnation."

As exciting as it all was, it was also a little unnerving. After all, who did they think was coming? It was only me. I was schlepping around the mall in my usual uniform: jeans, sweatshirt, purple tennies, earrings—always earrings—and lip gloss. My cowlick was sticking up on the back of my head, and I'd left my house in a total shambles. I was slurping a diet pop and downing a Mrs. Field's macadamia-nut-and-white-chocolate cookie, and there it was: "Meet the Author."

At any rate, as unnerving as it was, it was also quite exciting. So exciting, in fact, that I went back later in the day with my camera to capture the scene. Pretty humble act, huh?

But what fun. I had my friend Mar stand in front of the displays and point at them like Vanna on "Wheel of Fortune" when she turns the letters. We had quite the time; I believe in celebration. I knew this would all be over very quickly.

And then came the day of the signing. I figured I had better act respectable. And so I did.

Some of my friends came, because of course I'd phoned nearly everyone I knew within driving distance. Others purchased the book because sales clerks steered them toward it. Some had seen the poster earlier in the week and actually came to get a signed copy for their moms. But one incident is permanently etched on my heart. I had never thought about the worthiness of *Don't Miss Your Kids!* until that moment.

Since I was posted fairly close to the doorway, I could entertain myself by people-watching, which proved fascinating even if the people weren't looking for me, and most weren't. In the midst of the busyness, in came a father with three children. He had a wee one on his hip, a toddler in tow and one about five years old holding the toddler's hand. They were all blond and beautiful. The father announced to them that they were here to buy Mom her Mother's Day gift. And the search began.

The oldest child suddenly spotted the rack of my books on display next to where I was standing. "Here it is!" she exclaimed. "That's the one Mommy wants!"

"Are you sure?" queried Dad.

"Yes, I'm sure."

I will never know where the mother had seen or heard about my book. Perhaps she'd been in the store with the children earlier in the week and scanned it. Maybe she'd heard one of my radio interviews or seen an article in one of the local papers. It really doesn't matter. What matters is the precious way the father approached his gift-buying task.

He picked up one of my books and showed it to each child, even the one on his hip who had no idea what he was talking about. "This is what we're going to get for Mommy," he quietly said. He knelt down, balancing the baby, and carefully showed the middle child. He was explaining that Mom wanted it, as well as seeking each child's approval. Their shopping expedition was obviously a mission of love.

Although I believed my book to be a good book with an important and freeing message, I had never considered its worthiness as a gift. Here it was, being sought not just to meet a Mother's Day obligation but as a precious, carefully chosen gift. A special gift. Just the right one for Mommy.

"Oh Lord," I silently prayed, "please let this book be worthy." Fighting back tears, I felt very small in the face of this love.

I will never know if Mom liked the book. In fact, I can't even be sure the little girl got it right; maybe it wasn't my book Mom really wanted. Of course pride and sincere good wishes want to think that it was and that she did. Still, this incident humbled me before God.

Did my humbling show? I doubt it. How could it? I stood there pen in hand, waiting to sign my name on the inside of a book already bearing my name. Right on the front, across the very top. In inch-tall red letters.

* * *

Although I do feel pride in my book, oddly enough I often

don't feel guilty about that. After all, as Ecclesiastes says, what more can one want than to be happy in one's labor? For goodness sake, even Paul began his letters in the Bible with a byline. *Paul* was the first word he usually wrote.

If we don't feel good about what we're doing, why do it? If we're embarrassed to put our name on it, maybe we ought to be rethinking whatever it is we're doing. Again, this whole thing tickles the edges of the self-esteem dilemma. Shouldn't we feel good about ourselves and our labors?

Donald W. McCullough, in *Finding Happiness in the Most Unlikely Places,* helped me sort through this issue of pride and self-esteem in relation to humility.

Nowadays pride assumes an honored place in the Most Admired Human Characteristics Hall of Fame. Advertisers appeal to material pride, psychiatrists massage limping pride, politicians promote national pride, civil-rights leaders cultivate racial pride, coaches incite team pride, business leaders promote civic pride, we all nurse wounded pride. What's wrong with pride?

First, a distinction. Not all pride is bad. Common sense makes room for a wholesome pride, the pride, say, a craftsman feels after months of creating an end table with perfectly joined corners and a finish you can use as a mirror. The pride of accomplishment can't be bad or God would be the first sinner; after six days of fashioning a universe, the Bible tells us, the Creator admired the result and said, "Very good." Perhaps we shouldn't even use the word *pride* in this sense. What we are really describing in this case is the pleasure of work well done. It's no sin to enjoy, with gratitude and a feeling of achievement, the fruit of careful labor—whether it be a great football team or a humane city or a magnificent universe.[1]

Thanks, guy. I needed that. Truly I did.

* * *

So what do humble people look like? John 15:16 tells us that Christ chose us and appointed us to go and bear fruit. Could fruit, then, be a sign of a truly humble person? "By their fruit you will recognize them" (Mt 7:20).

I once heard Paul Thigpen speak on "The Humble Writer" at a Christian writers' conference. He said, "Humility is the soil in which the fruit of the Spirit and gifts of the Spirit grow."

Paul prays in Colossians that the holy and faithful people of God at Colossae may bear fruit. Here's what he has to say:

> For this reason, since the day we heard about you, we have not stopped praying for you and asking God to fill you with the knowledge of his will through all spiritual wisdom and understanding. And we pray this in order that you may live a life worthy of the Lord and may please him in every way: bearing fruit in every good work, growing in the knowledge of God, being strengthened with all power according to his glorious might so that you may have great endurance and patience, and joyfully giving thanks to the Father, who has qualified you to share in the inheritance of the saints in the kingdom of light. (Col 1:9-12)

Paul's qualifications for bearing fruit seem to be spiritual wisdom, understanding, a life worthy of the Lord.

Don't underestimate the importance of wisdom in Paul's list. James says that the wisdom that comes from heaven is "first of all pure; then peace-loving, considerate, submissive, full of mercy and good fruit, impartial and sincere" (Jas 3:17). Now we're getting somewhere. All these attributes are hard to muster on any consistent basis without the power from within. But all of them definitely show.

Peter says that the humble in spirit give blessing (1 Pet 3:8-9). Certain people come to my mind when I read that—friends who always make me feel blessed when I spend time with them or chat with them on the phone. They are sincere people, seeking people, liberal with compliments and encouragement. I'm not talking gushy and false, but real. I'm not talking perfect either, but real. The humility of these people does show, and I seek them out.

Peter also says that when you give blessing, you inherit it for yourself as well. It occurs to me that the people I know who give the most blessings believe themselves to be the most blessed. Hm.

Back to my *Tribune* clips. Remember someone wrote that her most humbling experience was working with the Special Olympics. I believe some of our purest examples of love and humility are given to us by people with Down's syndrome. In fact, when Chris Burke, who plays Corky Thatcher on "Life Goes On," was highlighted in the "Fast Track" column, he made a statement that may be the epitome of humility. When asked, "What three words best describe you?" he said: "I love you."

One of the most beautiful articles I have ever read, "Life-long Children Who Teach," appeared in the October 2, 1991, issue of *The Lutheran* magazine. Gary L. Bradshaw, whose daughter, Angela, has Down's syndrome, wrote of his experience at the Special Olympics.

He didn't really want to be there; he had "work to be done, deadlines to meet, orders to be placed, money to be made. I didn't have time for this," he says at the beginning of the article. But, he admits, his "sour mood never had a chance. Warmth greater than the sun slowly enveloped me. As I watched the athletes, their inextinguishable joy washed over me. And it slowly dawned on me that they had a firmer grip on reality than I did. They were secure." He continues:

Huggers were everywhere, sharing love with each competitor as they finished their race. Some cheated and hugged more than one.

I never had a chance. I became swept up in the emotion, the love that permeated the festivities. The competitors were hugging each other, the coaches, the volunteers, even the stadium employees who were hauling trash.

Their courage was incredible. Some of them could hardly walk, yet they could run. They would stop and help one another. Their love of life and of those that filled their lives was more sincere than I had ever seen in my world of "normality." Maybe it was, after all, we "normal types" who were lacking.

Something warm covered my hand. Turning, I looked into the ebony eyes of a young African American girl who had a pink butterfly painted on her cheek. Clinging possessively to me, she rattled on incessantly for a half hour. I began to realize that she was unaware of our differences. I wished that I were the same. She laughed and chattered, then led the other children who surrounded me in 10 choruses of "Jesus Loves Me," a statement she knew to be true. And I also knew that Jesus loved me.

I saw my own little girl in a new light that day. Angela soon stood before me, ecstatic over her white ribbon—her reward for finishing fifth out of five competitors.

Angela has Down's syndrome. Conceived in love, Angela has become love's gift, and a giver of love also. She has touched more lives in a more positive way than I can ever hope to.

Angela loves God with all her heart and soul, and she loves music. She sings in the church choir, expressing that love in her extraordinary version of continual B-flat. Yet every fiber of her being goes into every word. I cannot say that I am always thankful when she sings, but then I do not always appreciate the beauty in a rose either.

Something special happens between Angela and older people, an interaction of love, a provision of mutual need. She responds to their gentleness and suffers her greatest pain when they are hurting.

She has taken more than her share of abuse from "normal" children, but she has never struck back. When she has taken all that she cares to, she merely goes elsewhere. It's as if she considers it their loss—not hers. I tend to agree. . . .

The thing that she seems to do best is to enjoy every minute, every second of life, loving everyone who will let her, eating whenever she can and making me feel like I am the most wonderful person in the world.

Angela possesses a love-saturated soul. She and her friends are lifelong children who teach. They have taught me that God expects each of us to become the best that we can possibly be as ordinary people before he makes us into anything else. That achievement alone would be truly uncommon.

That first Special Olympics was several years ago. Angela is a teenager now. She has won gold, bronze and silver medals, but she seems to love her ribbons the most. God tells us that we shall be made perfect and whole in the life to come. The vision of Angela in a state of perfection thrills me. But I wonder if God really has much improvement to make in her.[2]

Does humility show? You tell me.

* * *

"Dear children, let us not love with words or tongue but with actions and in truth" (1 Jn 3:18). In Matthew 6:1-3, however, Jesus gives us stern warnings about how we are to perform deeds of love.

Be careful not to do your acts of righteousness before men, to be seen by them. If you do, you will have no reward from your Father in heaven.

So when you give to the needy, do not announce it with trumpets, as the hypocrites do in the synagogues and on the streets, to be honored by men. I tell you the truth, they have received their reward in full. But when you give to the needy, do not let your left hand know what your right hand is doing, so that your giving may be in secret. Then your Father, who sees what is done in secret, will reward you.

Jesus goes on in the next few verses to tell us to pray in secret as well. And then to forgive and fast in secret.

What does this mean? That if we're really leading a humble life, no one will ever see it or know it? Sounds like a possibility. And it seems quite clear that being seen shouldn't be our motive. Remember, though, that Jesus and his disciples did nearly all their works of healing and mercy in public. Thus it would seem that attitude and motivation are crucial. We should not act "to be honored by men" but for the glory of God.

On the other hand, doesn't Scripture tell us that God can even use evil intentions for good (Ex 50:20)? Sometimes we do act in pride, but though our prideful behavior may keep us from being personally blessed, God is often gracious to use our mistakes to benefit ourselves and others in spite of our intentions and motives.

* * *

A dear friend of mine has been suffering terribly with a disease that causes her much pain and loss of energy. As I found when I broke my leg, illness has a way of getting your attention. But Donna's suffering will not end when a cast comes off.

She has thrashed through much questioning and anguish in the past couple of years; there was even a point when death seemed the answer. But by grace, she says she has finally stopped fighting and is learning to live with her circumstances. This doesn't mean she has total peace, but life is better.

In fact, her perception of herself and her role in the world are being transformed. At the beginning of her illness, she said over a soul-baring lunch one day, "I was so worried and caught up in what was happening to me that I didn't see anything else in the whole world." By grace and through counseling with a friend and reading, she began to heal emotionally. Then she realized that she needed to think about more than herself.

She said the illness has made her more able to accept people just as they are rather than imposing expectations on them. She teaches elementary English and has found her approach to her work affected by her spiritual growth. Now I can't imagine that she was ever anything other than patient and loving; these are her natural gifts. But I could see in her eyes and tell in her voice that something more was bubbling within her.

She told of a student who made her cry. The little girl wasn't doing very well on an assignment—and apparently her entire self-concept was shaky. "If you could see me on roller skates," she said to my friend, her teacher, "then you could see how good I am."

"Yes, I am teaching a subject and I care about that subject," Donna said. "But when the children walk out of my class, I want them to learn to feel real good about themselves. I want them to feel and believe the message that I accept them the way they are. I felt so bad she didn't know that."

* * *

"If you could see me on roller skates, then you could see how good I am."

Dear Jesus, if you could only see me when no one else does, in those quiet times when my heart is humming your love for others. If you could know how much I love you and how I want to be good, but sometimes just can't seem to be. If you could search my heart and know my earnest desire to snuggle close to you and feel your presence, even when I'm dark inside. If you could just help me show the love I feel for other people. Help me show it even when they act bad, because I often act bad too. Even though I don't mean to. Even though I don't want to. If you could see me when I dance for joy around the house because I'm so happy I know you.

If I could only remember that you do. See me. Know me. And love me. Always. Just like I am.

Amen. Your child, Char the Star.

* * *

One Sunday our pastor, Friend Rod, gave a sermon titled "See What the Lord Can Do." Here is an excerpt:

A pastor ended his sermon one Sunday morning by inviting those people to come forward who wanted to accept Christ as their Lord and Savior. A steady stream of people responded, with arms lifted high in praise and thanksgiving. And among those who came forward was a woman of great wealth and high social standing. Each person was given an opportunity to make a testimony to their new faith, and this is what that woman said:

"I want you to know why I came forward this morning. It's not due to any word spoken by the preacher. It's not due to any of you in this congregation. Rather, I am here because of a woman you don't even know. Her fingers are roughened by toil, and the hard work of many years has stooped her low. She is just a cleaning woman who has served me in my home for many years. I have never known her to become impatient. I have never known her to speak an unkind word or do anything dishonorable. But I do know of countless little acts of unselfish love that adorn her life.

"I'm ashamed to say it, but I have openly sneered at her faith and criticized her unquestioning dedication. Yet when my daughter died, this woman helped me more than anyone else. She listened to me. She cried with me. And finally she helped me to look beyond the grave, and to shed my first tears of faith and hope. The gentle magnetism of her life has drawn me to her Lord. I want for myself what has made her life so beautiful."

"And we, who with unveiled faces all reflect the Lord's glory, are being transformed into his likeness with ever-increasing glory, which comes from the Lord, who is the Spirit" (2 Cor 3:18).

Perhaps the veil is pride. And when pride is set aside, when we unveil, God's glory shines through us, loving others into the kingdom.

* * *

Does humility show? Yes. And when it does, what shows is not anything we do or don't do; it has nothing to do with us. It is God himself shining through us. What shows is the face of God.

Can we be walking in humility and be aware of it at the same time? I believe so, if what we are aware of is the love of God that quenches our thirst as it flows through us to others.

Do I believe this with all my being? I do. Does it disagree with Scripture? Not that I've found. Remember, God calls us to humility. He modeled it. He empowers us from within. He enables us to accomplish everything that he calls us to do.

"Now to him who is able to do immeasurably more than all we ask or imagine, according to his power that is at work within us, to him be glory in the church and in Christ Jesus throughout all generations, for ever and ever! Amen" (Eph 3:20-21). A Scripture always worth repeating, and so I have.

7

The
Pie-Slinging
Blues

I'VE talked about cream pies, humble pies, cow pies, apple pies and a few other pies I didn't apply descriptive labels to. Right now, though, I'd simply like to invite you to a pie-slinging contest. Any type of pie is fair game for the lively center-ring action in the stories that follow.

Notice the differences in the way they land. See the responses. Notice that each pie is preceded by vanity.

Please stay and help clean up the mess; it gets pretty slippery out there. There's an extra reward for those who do.

* * *

Once upon a time there was an upcoming wedding and the bride-to-be wanted to look lovely—right down to the ends of her fingers.

The problem was that the bride chewed her nails. And this wedding happened quite a while ago, in the Pre-Acrylic Era. Back then long nails were reserved for the likes of ladies who didn't have to deal with typing, girdles or opening their own car doors. Remember, this was quite a while ago.

Anyhow, Charlene the bride, in a desperate attempt to hide her bad habit, decided to disguise her nubbies with glue-on glamour from Walgreens. One of the main reasons for this effort was so she could forever cherish the traditional hand-on-hand photograph that would someday adorn her fireplace mantel.

The wedding went fine. But by the time the meal was over, the cake was cut and family members were ready to take the hand-on-hand photos, Charlene, in her exuberant joy, had managed to knock off all the nails except two: the ones on her middle and index fingers of her right hand.

With a burst of creative thinking, she gently placed her two delicately extended fingers atop her beloved's masculine (size 13 ring) hand, softly tucking the rest of her fingers into his palm. But the family photographer stood a tad too far away, so that the developed photo suggested that his tripod had slipped. In fact, the glossy showed the peace symbol against a backdrop of two headless people.

Years later, Charlene, in a fit of vanity before an upcoming vacation, once again made the decision for nails. Since her now-you-have-them-now-you-don't wedding nails had left an everlasting vacant spot on her mantel, this time she opted for a manicurist's weekly assistance in growing her own.

Enter Tonya, a hair stylist and manicurist in a local beauty salon. Tonya encouraged Charlene by filing, shaping and massaging her budding nails. Tonya asked little in return.

"Don't put your thumb in the soak," she requested. You see, Tonya had just painstakingly Superglued a nasty snag, and it needed time to dry.

Charlene rested her right hand (Hand No. 1) in the soap-filled container, which looked like the gum line in a king-sized upper plate. Her thumb lay safely outside the warm soap.

While Tonya worked on Charlene's other hand (Hand No. 2), the two chatted and hummed to the music that was being piped in over the salon speakers. Tonya soon discovered that the fingernail on the ring finger of this hand (No. 2) needed a glue job too. She handled the task with ease.

While Charlene intently watched the near-surgical procedure, the thumb of Hand No. 1 mysteriously slipped into the warm sudsy soak before the glue was dry. It was the one thing Tonya had asked her not to do.

"That's okay," Tonya said. "I'll just do it over." While Tonya was repeating the repair, the ring finger of Charlene's left hand (No. 2), all on its own, folded under, thereby gluing itself to the towel.

Tonya didn't even sigh. She simply picked the terrycloth out of the glue with tweezers and once again repaired a repair.

Thanks to Tonya's relentless patience, saintly perseverance and dedication, the manicure was finally completed. Then Charlene, having had her hands in warm water for so long, found that she needed to use the rest-room.

There are no words to describe the contortions one must perform to peel a pair of jeans off a body when one's fingers are adorned with wet nail polish.

Ultimately, ten pretty nails prevailed—for at least a couple of hours. But one has to wonder where vanity will draw the line.

In case you didn't notice, this was a peach pie: it came in slices.

* * *

Once upon a time a woman named Charlene lost a lot of weight. She was feeling very good about herself. Too good, you might say. In fact, she spent much of her time thinking about herself, and just how good she looked.

On this particular day, Charlene was driving into town to do errands in the family sedan, blasting the radio (tuned in to a very hip station for a midlifer) with the windows down, so that the breeze could blow through her ever-so-cute hair and twirl around her cute little self. The rear-view mirror gave repeated testimonies to just how cute, chic and young she was looking.

Then she saw him: the hitchhiker. He was a friend of her high-school-aged son and no doubt on his way back to school. Squealing the brakes (she knew she could because she was within seconds of having checked her rear-view mirror), she pulled over and offered him a ride. He happily accepted and hopped in.

Charlene accelerated very quickly, the way a youth might do were he or she driving a hot car with a big engine. She turned the radio up just one more notch to bring home the fact that she was ever-so-cool to be listening to such a hip station. And of course, I've already said how teeny, tiny and cute she was.

"What are these?" her son's friend asked.

"What?" Charlene asked, turning her cute little head his way and flashing him her cute little smile.

To Charlene's horror, he was holding up the Tupperware container of plastic bingo chips she had taken to bingo the night before. Not cool. Tupperware and bingo chips were definitely not cool.

Splat. Mincemeat. She was picking the little wads off her too-cute little self for the rest of the day.

* * *

Once upon another day Charlene woke up and everything just seemed to fall into place. It was one of those days when your orange juice tastes extra sweet, the morning news isn't too terrible and your hair slicks right into place. Your face isn't puffy and your favorite outfit isn't in the laundry and the sun is shining brightly. What more could woman or man want?

Charlene had several items to pick up, so she chose one of those universal types of stores that carry it all. Upon entering, she smiled and said "Good morning" to the people behind the cash registers near the door. They smiled back.

She selected a cart and wheeled it around. The cart didn't even have a wobbly wheel. Isn't life grand? She twirled it from aisle to aisle, popping in item after item, although twice she had to ask for assistance to locate the exact item that was on sale. Each person who helped her returned her smiles.

Finally, she checked out, chattering all the while to the

cashiers who were smiling, smiling, smiling back at her. They discussed what a good bargain one particular item was, so she quickly ran back through the store for "just one more." Then she headed for her car, humming all the while.

After unloading the goodies into her trunk, she hopped behind the wheel and cranked up the engine. Making a quick check in the rear-view mirror, she discovered, to her astonished horror, that she only had *one lens in her sunglasses.*

Ice cream pie. No doubt about it. Cold and rude awakening.

By the way, if you find it hard to believe that a person wouldn't notice that she or he is only wearing one colored lens, try it sometime. Your eyes simply adjust. Also ponder *how utterly ridiculous and stupid you look.* No wonder all the sales clerks were smiling, smiling, smiling back at Charlene.

* * *

Now the moral to be gleaned from this pie-slinging contest is probably obvious: "Pride goes before destruction, a haughty spirit before a fall" (Prov 16:18). But there is also a hope-filled lesson of humility: "The LORD upholds all those who fall and lifts up all who are bowed down" (Ps 145:14).

You see, humility begins after we are washed up from the mess and we realize that only God's mercy and justification and all-encompassing love enable us to become squeaky-clean again. It is when we are bowed down in God's glorious presence and love that he lifts us once more, rendering us whiter than snow (Ps 51:7).

It isn't the pie that transforms us. The pie is simply the attention-getter, and attention it gets, although not the kind we were looking for when pride, like an industrial-strength pie-attracting magnet, drew the pie toward our face. No; the pie is nothing. God is what matters—God and his anointing, cleansing bath. In the warmth of the soothing water we begin to learn about humility. We realize that God loves us, even when we are dripping with pie.

A holy pie can't do us any good, though, when we refuse to accept the goodness that comes with the package. Instead we grumble and complain and blame it on someone else. We stop with the mess and do not allow the cleanup. Or we refuse to acknowledge that there was even a pie at all. In that case, we turn our backs on it—and so our backsides are quickly adorned with more gooey pies. These are the lightest of pies because we don't even feel them. Problem is, everyone knows we're wearing them but us.

* * *

So here we are in the aftermath of the pie-slinging contest. I hope you stayed for the cleanup. If you're like me, you'd usually rather skip out and let somebody else handle that part. But this time the cleanup was the best part of the fun. Isn't that just like God? What a fooler he is.

I don't think it would be fair to have brought you to the contest, however, if I didn't introduce you to the participants. No, not the recipient of the pies; she has already been revealed. I'm talking about the pie slingers, and notice I used the plural there.

Thus far we have moved under the assumption that God is the one who slings the pies. Certainly he slings the *holy* pies. But I wonder if he slings all of the pies. After all, Satan is always lurking around trying to make us believe things that are untrue, father of lies that he is. Maybe he zings some in there. Unholy pies. Are we to accept them? And how do we know the difference? Will they taste the same?

Will some of our humbling experiences reveal the light and some scorch us? Will some teach us lessons and some lead us astray?

I remember a time when I was baby-sitting. I was in eighth grade, and I hated baby-sitting. All my friends did it, though, so I'd decided I might as well too, although not so often that I couldn't have any fun in life.

Anyway, the house where I was sitting was exactly a quarter of a mile down the road from mine. I know this because the kids used to drag race that strip. So I wasn't that far from home, but I wasn't in the security of my home either. And being the type of person I was, I wanted to please the kiddies if it was at all possible and within the realm of reason. Or at least within this immature eighth-grader's realm of immature reason. And so I obliged the children with ghost stories in their upstairs bedrooms. And I'm a very good ghost-story teller, even though I don't like scary things. Especially since I'm more mature now.

The problem was that once the story was over, I had to go back downstairs. Alone. I slowly made my way down the enclosed stairway. Quickly, I slipped onto the couch right next to the brightest lamp in the living room. The house was perfectly still because I had turned the television off before I scooted the kids upstairs.

And then I heard it. A very strange yet subtle sound, coming from the front of the house. The sound someone might make if he were, say, trying to pry open a window.

With a big knife.

I sat there with my heart racing at two-forty until I thought it would burst. Finally, I decided I simply had to get up and look—okay, peek—out the window just to put my mind at ease so I could say, "See, there's nobody there. Now turn up the television *real loud* and forget about it." Slowly to the window I crept. With quivering fingers I lifted one slat of the venetian blinds and . . .

Yikes! Two huge eyes were looking right back at me! I yelped, hurled myself back from the window and began to hyperventilate.

And then it dawned on me that the two eyeballs had been mine. They were nothing more than my own reflection.

Possibility three: Do we fling our own pies? There's that old adage, you know: When you are pointing a finger at someone, just remember that there are three more pointing back at you. Try it right now; it's true.

"Whoever trusts in his riches will fall" (Prov 11:28). "A house divided against itself will fall" (Lk 11:17). "If you have played the fool and exalted yourself, or if you have planned evil, clap your hand over your mouth!" (Prov 30:32). Of course a pie would do just fine too.

"And we know that in all things God works for the good of those who love him, who have been called according to his purpose" (Rom 8:28). Whether an embarrassing experience was good or bad, God can use it for our good. But does that mean he dealt it?

* * *

I have several collections of things. Most of the items are not worth more than five bucks. They are simply things I like looking at. Glass blobs; old inkwells (symbolic for a writer); pigs—even though I don't want them, people assume I do because I have them, so they get me more; things with watermelon wedges painted on them; earrings, lots of earrings.

When you have so much stuff, some of it occasionally gets broken. Should one of my precious things hit the floor and shatter, as occasionally happens, do I consider that since God loves me he needed to send me a holy pie to temper my pride in my collections and diminish my inclination to hoard? Do I blame the devil for tempting me with all those things? Do I own responsibility for having no self-control?

I suppose the answer could be yes. To all of the above.

Is God slinging pies at innocent children when they contract deadly diseases? Of course not. It would be hard to broach this subject without taking a look at Job. Job who could have considered that the heavens had indeed rained pies on him.

Job was an upright man, and God had blessed him. "He had seven sons and three daughters, and he owned seven thousand sheep, three thousand camels, five hundred yoke of oxen and five hundred donkeys, and had a large number of servants. He was the greatest man among all the people of the East" (Job 1:2-3).

Job was feeling as though he were the target in a cosmic game of darts between God and the devil. His property was either ruined or stolen, and his family killed. He was covered with boils, and he sat in a big pile of ashes, surrounded by critical friends and a nagging wife. He had a lot to talk to God about.

Pretty good roundup by Joni Eareckson Tada. What I love

even more than her picturesque roundup, however, is the way she nails what is important about this. Job didn't pray, " 'Oh that I might be healed of these boils,' or 'Oh, that I might have my children back,' or even, 'Oh, that these friends and my wife would get off my back!' Instead Job's desire was to see the Father's face and feel His smile."[1]

"If only I knew where to find him; if only I could go to his dwelling! I would state my case before him and fill my mouth with arguments. I would find out what he would answer me, and consider what he would say" (Job 23:3-5).

Job had collected a lot of things that he might lose. And we know God allowed Satan to sift Job, so the battle between light and darkness was being waged here.

Jesus, too, was tempted by the devil. In fact, he was led by the Spirit into the desert for that purpose (Mt 4:1). But what is more important is that God loved Jesus, and God loved Job. God knew all Job's struggles, allowed the sifting, then "blessed the latter part of Job's life more than the first. He had fourteen thousand sheep, six thousand camels, a thousand yoke of oxen and a thousand donkeys. And he also had seven sons and three daughters" (Job 42:12-13).

Job was a godly man. He loved the Lord with all his heart. Many sufferings befell him, but he kept himself pointed toward God, even when what he wanted to do most was plead his case before him. It was God Job wanted to talk to. Regardless of who had caused his suffering, Job wanted to talk to God.

And God allows our humility, too, to be tested. At the end of the wilderness wanderings Moses said to the Israelites, "Remember how the LORD your God led you all the way in the desert these forty years, to humble you and to test you in order to know what was in your heart, whether or not you would keep his commands" (Deut 8:2).

Sometimes we need to be humbled in order to learn. Does it matter who trips the trigger that sends a pie our way?

Andrew Murray encourages us to learn to see hardships and reproofs—whether deserved or not—as opportunities to prove that "Jesus is all to us. . . . It is indeed blessed—the deep happiness of heaven—to be so free from self that whatever is said about us or done to us is lost and swallowed up in the thought that Jesus is all."[2]

What is humility apart from God anyway? It flat out doesn't seem to matter.

* * *

When I asked the man in the bookstore for books on the subject of humility and he responded that there weren't many and, after all, who would dare try and write about it, I suspected that I'd received a holy pie from God to remind me just who I was. After all, who was I to dare?

After much consideration, I have decided it wasn't God who slung that pie; it was Satan, planting the seed of doubt. After all, if I believe that I am a child of God, one of his very own, created for good works—and I do—then who am I *not* to write about humility, even if I'm hardly an expert? Who am I not to write about humility when I find I am concluding that humility is God's own nature? Who, then, would be most interested in keeping someone from exploring humility and light, if not the master of darkness?

Is fear of humiliation keeping me from doing what God has called me to do? Then it's a temptation, and I need to set my eyes on Christ and ignore the pie.

Maybe it does matter who slings the pies. It certainly matters whether we accept them or not—especially if they will keep us from spreading the Word.

8

Humbling
Awe

AND being found in appearance as a man, he humbled himself and became obedient to death—even death on a cross!" (Phil 2:8).

Think of it. Jesus Christ, the only begotten son of God, humbled and emptied himself in obedience—for us! For me. For Char the Star.

Sometimes there are no humbling pies. Sometimes the awareness of God's power and undying love for us sweeps into our souls with such magnificent bounty that we can do nothing but let ourselves be filled with awe. No holy pies, just humbling awe.

Nature, by its very God-ordained power, overwhelms me with awe. The Grand Canyon. Yosemite in winter. The ocean, gently lapping on sand, delivering up tiny, intricately designed shells, then devastating communities with unleashed fury. The intoxicating fragrance of a pine forest. Giant waterfalls that spill over what seem to be the very edges of time and space, only to crash down the banks and end in tranquil, refreshing pools that soothe a heat-filled body.

God woos us with these strokes of his creative hand, even if we don't know that they come from him. Drawing us ever deeper into his wonder. Enabling us to ride an updraft in a hot-air balloon or wildly skitter down a toboggan run on the side of his mountain. Holding us close; backing us up so we can get the full effect of the view.

Paul Thigpen wrote about his questioning youth. Sometimes he wanted to believe in God, but other times he believed his thirst for another world was illusion. Often our teenage years slam us into this "lie of the world," as he puts it. And yet . . .

For me, the visible Machine surrounding us was the sum total of reality—no God, no spirits, no heaven, no life after death. At least, that's what my modern-educated mind insisted. But on rare occasions, usually unexpectedly, my heart rebelled.

How do I describe that rebellion? It always took place when I was alone. Once it was on a summer afternoon at the height of a sudden thunderstorm. Again, it happened on a spring morning when my ear caught the low moan of a mourning dove. It came several times at the beach as I listened to the deafening lullaby of the waves, and again when I once looked up to see the icy vastness of a clear sky on a winter night.

Each time, the sensation was the same. Beyond whatever sight or sound met me in the physical world, it was as if I heard what could only be called a single note played on a trumpet from a distant country. In such a moment I would fall motionless, arrested by the surpassing sweetness of that sound. And I ached so deeply to hear the entire melody that my eyes would moisten with homesickness for a Land I'd never seen. . . .

My Lord, if only I'd realized then that You were that Friend; that Your Song had soured over my noisy barricades and run me through. But those moments seemed a mockery, because I'd abandoned all hope of any Voice within the thunder, or any Face behind the clouds. I was a fool.[1]

Romans 1:20 reminds us that everyone has seen God's handiwork, his creation. None have excuse. Until we belong to him, our ears do not hear; our eyes do not see.

But God is there. God, always knocking. Surrounding us with his presence. Insistently rapping. Never giving up just because we don't realize it's him.

"Here I am! I stand at the door and knock. If anyone hears my voice and opens the door, I will come in and eat with him, and he with me. To him who overcomes, I will give the right to sit with me on my throne, just as I overcame and sat down with my Father on his throne" (Rev 3:20-21).

Funny thing about people. It's not that many of them don't believe in God, it's just that they're afraid it really is God at the door. And then what? What if it is?

Other times, angels deliver his message right into our laps. When we are about as low and hopeless as we can get, we seem to have no choice but to receive him and his bountiful love. Such was the case for me in 1975.

* * *

It was a few short weeks after Christmas, and life had resumed its routine. Bret was back in school after the long break; the Christmas stuff was finally tucked away in the attic. Cub Scouts was back in full swing. That was important in my life: I was a den mother, and a darn good one.

Then one night around 2:30 A.M., the shrill ring of the phone pierced our sleep, setting our hearts racing. George answered, but I could tell that whatever he was hearing, it wasn't good, and it had to do with me. Finally, after several agonizing moments, he handed me the phone.

It was my father's voice I heard. Mom had had a heart attack, he said. She was in the hospital. The doctors didn't know if they could keep her going. Better come. They just didn't know.

"Better come" was more than it seemed. We were in Illinois; Mom was in Albuquerque, New Mexico.

What do you do with your children in the middle of the night? Where do you get money for airline tickets? How do you hang onto sanity during an agonizing plane ride when you don't know if your mother will be dead or alive when the plane lands?

I racked my brain to recall my last conversation with Mom. Was it happy? Was there unfinished business? Did these thoughts mean I had no hope?

Somehow George and I managed to arrive at the Albuquerque airport before noon. My brother met us. The doctors had discovered that Mom had suffered a stroke as well as the heart attack; it wasn't clear at that point which had come first. She was alive and in intensive care. We could see her for only five minutes each hour. She wasn't conscious, and she was full of life-support equipment. These are the facts my brother delivered on that miserable drive to the hospital. He was glad we were there, he said. I wasn't sure.

When I entered Mom's hospital room for the first time, it was with more fear than I had ever experienced. She looked foreign to me. Her eyes were closed, and her mouth was open and filled with a ventilator tube. Things went up her nose and down her throat. Things were stuck in her arms and monitoring her heart. Things. Awful things. Cold, icy, foreign things infiltrating a mother who was nothing but warmth.

There was nothing to do but stand and stare. It was as though she wasn't really there; it was as if evil itself had consumed her body and crept all over her skin. I could not touch her. I could barely breathe. I was glad when the time was up and my eyes could turn away from this sight, although the picture of her in that bed would not leave my mind.

I had only seen my mother this one time when a neurologist entered my family's small circle and slapped us. Hard. With the icy fingers of his cold voice.

"Here's the situation. It's just like someone has taken Nellie's head, chopped off the top, poured her brains on a cutting board and diced them up, then poured them back again. The scan shows that kind of damage to her communication center. She will never be more than a vegetable. I suggest you turn the machines off."

What a ruthless, uncaring creature he was. Obviously, he had no feelings, or had become numb to them to protect himself; still, that is never an excuse for cruelty. Before we'd had time to completely grasp what had happened to our mother, our wife, someone wanted us to pull her plug. No mercy. No kindness. No love. We were sickened. Grieved, confused, numb. It made no sense: the very life of the woman we loved, the woman who had fed and nurtured us, was now in our hands. Hands that were incapable of moving. Lips that were incapable of speech. Fear and anguish and anger consumed us.

"I'll let you think about it a while," the neurologist said. Then he disappeared down the hall.

I will flash you forward a few days in this story. We were, of course, unable to make that kind of decision on the spur of a precious life's moment. We were still digesting the fact that this was even reality and not a nightmare—yet it never ceased to be a nightmare. We did, praise God, hear several miracle stories from other patients' relatives who learned of our situation. Waiting areas can become intimate places. We clung to the hope of "That's what they told us too, but . . ."

Mom stayed the same. My father went back to work; my parents owned their own business, and economic difficulties ruled his choice. My brother disappeared for several days, unable to handle the situation. My husband eventually had to head back to his job and corral our children. I would not, could not leave.

My mother's mother and sister flew in and shared hospital sitting with me. They were both wrecks; one had to see her daughter, fruit of her womb, lying blank and helpless, punctured and probed; the other, my mom's only sibling, had always been emotionally weak and suffered from mental health problems. I perceived that I had to be the strong one. That was my job. Strength. Strength I tried to draw from myself. I railed against circumstances that had landed me so far away from friends and a support system.

It wasn't that I hadn't accepted Christ into my life as a child, and it wasn't that I didn't pray; but I did not know God intimately. I did not know how to turn things over. I'd had no practice letting go of life. And so it was myself I depended on. It was my strength that I believed had to carry everyone, including Mom.

I would wander the halls in a daze, often stopping at the east end of the building to stare at the Sandia Mountains through the huge glass windows. The mountains were so grand. So solid. So dependable. The more I looked at them, the more I found myself drawn to their beauty, ever changing, yet always the same. The sun rose orange and brilliant in the morning from behind their shelter; dusk turned them purple, majestic. Somehow I began to cling to the mountains, to their visual presence, their calm. Did I, like Paul Thigpen, hear the "single note played on a trumpet from a distant country" calling me from the maroon depths of those mountains?

One day, I found myself near the end of my strength, and God, in his timely, life-giving love, sent an angel named Dorothy Booker to my side. She found me sitting at the end of the hall, facing the mountain, doing macramé to keep myself busy. I instantly felt at home with this black, beautiful, very round, large-bosomed woman who called herself Dorothy

Booker and said she was there with her mother, and could I make her one of those plant hangers? That is how our conversation began.

Before it was over, I was pressed deep against her comforting breasts as I sobbed about my mother. I poured out the anguish over feeling that life and death were in my hands. I explained that I felt guilty for asking God to let Mom live if a vegetable was all she would be; I felt guiltier asking him to let her die. I believed it was I, not God, who had control over life and death. I simply didn't know better.

After my wrenching sobs subsided—but not the tears—Dorothy sat back and held out her hands in front of me. She cupped them side by side like a cradle.

"The Lord's got your mama right here in the palm of his hands, child. He loves her more than you can even imagine the word means. Ain't nothin' you can do to change that. If the Lord wants your mama to live and you pull the plug, no matter, she'll live. If it's time he called her home, she'll go, even if you don't pull the plug. Lord loves your mama, child. Ain't nothin' gonna happen to your mama he ain't in charge of. I tell you he's got her right here cradled in his palms, and he holds her close to his heart. He loves her, child, more than you. Let him do what's best; he will anyway. Turn her over. It's out of your hands and into his. It's in the Lord God Almighty's hands."

God's love for my mother and me poured straight through Angel Dorothy Booker and into my heart.

The situation did not immediately lose its intensity or its drama or its gut-wrenching heartache, but everything had changed. Even though I still combed the hair of a mother who didn't respond, a mother who suddenly and eerily had one eye open and one closed, even though I wept uncontrollably nearly every time I left the room, I saw God's arms around my mother. I saw her cradled in his hands and drawn as close to his bosom as I had been to Angel Dorothy's. He held us both very close.

Decisions were ultimately made; Mom lived for several days in spite of them; then, her body gave up; it was finished. But God loved her; God loved me. That was all I knew. That was all I needed to know. That was all I could handle at that time, but it was enough.

"I have much more to say to you, more than you can now bear. But when he, the Spirit of truth, comes, he will guide you into all truth" (Jn 16:12-13). I could have borne no more then. God knew it. The Spirit of truth never gives us more than we can handle.

God used the mountains and angels of Albuquerque to minister to me when I was at the end of myself. Humbling awe.

"I will lift up my eyes to the mountains; from whence shall my help come? My help comes from the Lord, who made heaven and earth" (Ps 121:1-2 NASB). I didn't even know that Scripture then. Imagine my awe when I first read it.

On my next visit to New Mexico I tried to find Dorothy Booker. The phone number I had didn't exist, nor did her address. Perhaps she came straight from heaven. I will never know. Although actually I do.

* * *

Humbling awe arrives in the face of death, but it also penetrates and fills the gift of life. I saw the miracle of God's creation in the birth of my sons. But Beth and John witnessed something even more magnificent in the adoption of their daughter. Let me start from the beginning. All names have been changed in this story.

Some years ago, during John and Beth's engagement, doctors discovered that John had testicular cancer. Surgery and chemotherapy followed, and so did the wedding plans. Beth said, "It was a gift from God that John survived." The doctors pronounced him cured. Beth and John were told they would likely never have children, but that didn't seem so bad at the time; new love flourished and the gift of John's life was enough.

"Once we were married, however," Beth said, "it didn't take too long, since I was already in my thirties, until I began to feel a little out of step with our married peers; they all had children. It started to hit home what not being able to have children really meant to us."

John had banked sperm before his surgery, but the odds were very slim that pregnancy could come about. Procedures were done in hopes . . . but to no avail. "We tried all sorts of things," said Beth. It wasn't to be. After about a year and a half of marriage, they decided to try and adopt. They were told they had to be married three years before a formal application could be made. The waiting began, and went on and on. The desire for children grew stronger. So did Beth's downward emotional spiral.

"About two years into it, I started to really grieve the impossibility of having my own children. That's something I had been counseled I would go through." In fact, the adoption-agency counselors wanted to make sure Beth and John did walk through this grief. Social workers want to be sure that adoptive parents have a healthy attitude toward adopting children, and they won't unless they have grieved the lack of their own biological children.

Beth said, "I had read the books about grieving and said, 'Oh, I'll never do this.' Was I ever humbled, because a year or two later, here I was curled up in my bed sobbing my eyes out for hours at a time. Uncontrollably. And no one could console me." But finally, she said, "I started to turn the corner and say, 'I will now hope for what God has for me.' "

It was in January that I first met Beth. She was leading a Bible study at my church. The study dealt with powerful emotions like fear and worry. Each member of the group was dealing with some degree of trauma: illness, aging, parents with cancer, an approaching deadline for a book (guess who), recent unemployment and childlessness. Weekly we met, reviewed our Bible study materials and shared what we had learned. What the Scriptures had revealed to us. How God was working in our lives.

Beth was quite open about the struggles that she and John were going through. Even though I have always been thankful for my children, I became even more thankful after hearing pieces of her story. I could not, cannot imagine such pain. Such unfulfilled longing.

During the few short weeks of our study, Beth shared how spring seemed to finally be dawning in her life. After all the years of waiting and setbacks and yearning—including having to reapply for adoption after a move, thus beginning the process anew because conditions vary from state to state, even within the same agency—healing was sprouting within her. "Finally in my heart I wasn't troubled anymore. I had been so troubled for a long time," she confessed.

And her healing was real. She wore it on her face. Her face actually became transformed during those weeks as I watched her and listened to her share the innermost parts of herself.

Yes, spring was dawning in her life. It was as visible and as welcome as the brilliant clutches of crocus that dare to bloom even through melting snow.

And the transformation was more than the hope of a child. Beth said with firm conviction that she was not sure a child would ever be in their lives, but whatever God did have in his plans for John and her, it was going to be good. She could sense it. Whatever it was, she was finally prepared and eager for God to reveal it. She had let go.

She was looking for a job and taking piano lessons because she believed the Lord was prompting her to do some things that would accelerate the healing process. "Regardless of what God has for you," she knew deep within her soul, "you can relax and finally loosen the tension in the back of your neck. You can relax and say, 'God is for you, he is not against you. He is going to work it out.' " Whatever "it" was to be.

The last Monday our study group met, Beth and I were the only two in attendance. We didn't actually study; we simply fellowshipped, and our conversation was lively and warm. I was sharing the great, humbling and exhausting things God was teaching me through the reading, prayer, meditation, research and writing of this book (he always teaches me through my writing); Beth was positively beaming with the sprouting hope of God's good work in her life.

That very afternoon a call came from the social worker at the adoption agency. "A young girl has chosen you," Beth and John were told. They learned that the mother was in the hospital, a week past due, and her doctor was about to induce labor. There would be a seventy-two-hour waiting period before any legal documents could be signed. She could still change her mind.

They had been chosen. Was it too much to believe? When Beth first told me this story, many of the Scriptures about God's chosen people came to my mind.

Chosen. Chosen by the birth parents from several case histories to be the adoptive parents to their child. If the birth parents stuck by that decision. The counselors believed they would. They said the mother was strong-willed; she had been counseled extensively and she had come to her own decision to do this. No coercion. But for seventy-two hours she would be with her baby.

Little by little, pieces of information were revealed. The birth parents were young: she was eighteen and he was nineteen. They had both been in counseling for months. Their parents were supportive. No drugs were involved.

A girl was born. Healthy. Complete. Whole. She would be in the arms of her birth mother for at least the next three days.

Some people advised John and Beth not to prepare for her, this baby for whom they had been chosen. If John and Beth made physical preparations for her and she didn't arrive, these friends said, it would be as though their first child had died. Nevertheless, John and Beth hauled out a crib they had long ago acquired and tucked away—just in case. They painted it and set it up in what they hoped would be their daughter's room.

Beth's mother and sister volunteered to do some shopping for diapers and other necessities; mothers themselves, they knew how to prepare. John and Beth made the decision to invest in a car seat. After all, they couldn't bring her home if they didn't have one. And they wouldn't know for sure if they had a child until Thursday evening; Friday morning she would be theirs. Maybe.

John and Beth prayed for three days for the birth mother and her daughter. A child John and Beth had already named in their hearts: Michelle. In fact, their lawyer had to have the name by Thursday morning because of the direct placement. They had turned in a name for a child they were not certain would be theirs.

In the midst of their aroused hopes and preparations, they still turned the child over to God. "We just said, 'What's best for Michelle, Lord. And if it's best for her to be with her mommy and daddy who gave her life, then you know that. If it's best for her to be with us to raise her to the glory of God, then you know that. It's your call.' "

And finally their phone rang. It was 11:30 on Thursday evening, hours after they thought they would hear. By this time, Beth was pretty sure that Michelle would not be theirs. "When the social worker said they had signed the papers, I was stunned," Beth says. "We just sat there. I said, 'That's great,' but I didn't feel great because it was so sobering."

The head of the agency explained that this had been the most emotional surrender the agency had ever taken. *Surrender*. That word again. Beth watches Michelle rock in her wind-up baby swing while she tells me this part of the story, her voice often cracking with emotion. "The social worker said, 'I think we really need to pray,' and so we prayed on the phone with the social worker for about twenty minutes. We were all crying. She said, 'This was a very, very tough time for these young people. As much as you want to be filled with joy, this is a time to remember them and what they have done, and you need to have that foremost in your mind when you go to get Michelle and meet them. They have asked to place her in your arms tomorrow, and you need to be praying that you will know what to say. As much as you want to be jumping up and down with joy—and they need to see your joy—you want to be sensitive to them and to the Holy Spirit.'"

John and Beth finally somewhat composed themselves, made several phone calls and then went shopping at an all-night grocery for bottles and formula. "We tried to go to sleep," Beth tells me. "But we couldn't."

The next morning, Beth and John waited in a room at the agency. The birth parents waited in another while the social worker picked Michelle up from the hospital. Then Michelle was placed in her birth parents' arms for the last time. They wept. Finally, they entered the room where John and Beth waited.

"With tears in their eyes, they came carrying Michelle to us," Beth says. "John and I immediately stood up, and John went to her and put his arms around her and the baby. The boy came over immediately and put his arms around me and gave me a big hug. That tells you a lot about this young man. Right away my first impression of him was 'mature, affectionate, kind-hearted.' About her," Beth said, choking back emotions, "I had no particular impression except grief. Grief was written all over her. She is a beautiful girl. I am old enough to be her mother—twenty-two years older. I looked at her and thought, *This could be my daughter.*

"We were all crying. She showed us Michelle, and I looked at her and said, 'She's beautiful.' " There were several awkward moments, then Beth asked how their parents were doing and acknowledged the fact that this must have been a most difficult week. There had been a death in the family, adding to the pain over the fact that a first grandchild was going to be given up. Everyone had held Michelle, including her birth grandparents. And now they were giving her over. Surrendering her. In pure love.

Pictures were taken with all four parents putting their hands on Michelle. The birth mother gave John and Beth a little toy for them to give to Michelle, and some nightgowns her mother had purchased. Finally this young, beautiful birth mother looked at her social worker and knew it was time to go. She said, "This is the last time I will see her, isn't it?" and began crying uncontrollably. She looked at Beth, put her hand on Michelle's head and said goodby. She asked John and Beth to never let Michelle forget her.

"There was a great deal of love in the room," Beth says, almost inaudibly. "These two young people understood unconditional love and they understood deep love. They left, and we just sat there sobbing. Grief and joy at the same time.

"That was when I became overwhelmed with this gift. That feeling of receiving something totally undeserved, totally a gracious gift, of looking into the Father's face and saying, 'You love me.' Pure, unconditional, undeserved love. When you really see that . . . there's joy, yes, but to me it was like looking at Calvary. I just sat there dumbfounded. I have never ever seen such sacrifice, and I don't think I ever will see such sacrifice in another human being.

"I looked at John and said, 'I don't deserve this,' and just wept. I looked at her tiny little hands and feet and said, 'Oh, she is more than anything we ever could have hoped for'— healthy mother, healthy family, good pregnancy, mature attitude about giving her up, wonderful things that we'll be able to tell Michelle about her birth parents. All of the counseling. The healthy little girl that she is. A baby need not be beautiful to be lovable, but her physical beauty did speak to me anyway of how God heaps it up and pours it all out. She looked placid lying there, like a picture of Jesus in the manger. Perfect little round mouth, beautiful complexion, peacefully sleeping in my arms, and I couldn't help but be totally humbled at this gift."

And then John and Beth's families poured into the room. Unbridled joy. Prayers. The passing around of this most precious gift.

Beth and I are both wet with tears, and she is now holding Michelle close in her arms. I am glad I brought my tape recorder to her home to capture this, because my hand long ago stopped writing anything decipherable.

Humbled. Undeserving. Loved. Awed.

Humbling awe.

* * *

There is a place near my home called the Morton Arboretum. It is 1500 acres of lush nature, one of the few places left in my area—perhaps the only one—where you can go to walk along twenty-five miles of path, depart from its course and be alone for quite some time. You could get lost in the woods, probably, if you wanted to. It's a place where you can seek refuge in nature. And so I did, one day.

It was a day of perfect weather; not too hot, not too cold. Jacketless, I set out on a path that leads around one of the lakes. After walking some time without coming across another human being—a circumstance that was just fine with me on this particular day—I nearly forgot that anyone other than myself existed.

But then I heard faint sounds of music—just a few notes that swirled around and blew by my ear. Then a couple more notes. Not a melody yet. I continued my journey, imagining the cosmonauts tethered in space and suddenly hearing a couple of notes, wondering if the rest of the song ended on another planet, another place in space.

I love music. It speaks to my soul. Music can change my moods, perk me up, draw out tears I need to release, even— and this is the most miraculous part—energize me to clean the house. Occasionally.

Anyway, here I was walking down this path in the arboretum, thinking about notes in space. And then a piece of a melody wafted by. No doubt about it; I was moving toward music. In fact, it was flute music.

My first inclination was to get a little prickly over the fact that someone was invading my solitude with a boombox. But then the string of notes came closer, and began to sound like . . . happy. Happy and real. Perhaps not a boombox at all.

I stopped. Was the music real or was it Memorex? Suddenly a little snippet from my past floated up. I was in fourth grade and I wanted to play the violin. But the violins were all taken, and the music teacher talked me into trying the flute. He said, in an accent I can no longer identify, "The flute makes b-e-a-u-t-i-f-u-l music." He sounded like music himself, just saying the word. His voice went up and down the scale at least four whole notes. And so I signed up for the flute and went home with one in a case.

Then I took it out to try it. And hated it. It wasn't a violin; it was a flute. I didn't like puckering my lips like that, although years later I must admit I found puckering to be quite enjoyable. Almost as enjoyable as music.

My flute-playing days were numbered. I didn't stick with it long. I never regretted giving the instrument up. With the mellowing of age, though, I did come to enjoy flute music. It often sounds like fairies dancing.

And so I stood still in the middle of the path in the arboretum, and the music came ever closer. I was sure fairies were dancing toward me, although they could not yet be seen. Their soulful yet light and freedom-filled tune brought a rush of joy into my spirit. I began moving toward the music, needing to be encompassed in its joy.

Then I saw him. A tall man wearing a funny hat and a reddish-brown beard. His mustache curled like a pageboy hairdo over his upper lip. He wore ragged pants, and his fingers were dancing—like fairies—on the slender silver flute that glistened when sunbeams filtered through the trees. His eyes twinkled. His entire presence seemed filled with joy—a joy that was escaping through his melody. It was a contagious joy. As he came closer, I began beaming. I became a fairy, dancing, walking, lilting through the forest.

And then he passed by. I didn't turn around and watch him disappear; I kept walking. Tears of joy spilled over my lower lashes as the tune slowly faded away.

* * *

"It is not sin that humbles us most, but grace," Andrew Murray said.[2] Lord, make us alive to the moments of humbling grace. The grace that enables us to be hugged by angels and dance with fairies and hold pure love in our arms.

9

Is There
Fun
After
Humility?

I WAS recently invited to speak at a women's retreat in Topeka, Kansas. The subject was sisterhood. Jane, the woman from Topeka who contacted me through InterVarsity Press, wanted to make sure that I would be willing to talk about getting real. Moving beyond judging by appearances. Ending competition with one another and focusing on lifting each other up.

"Yup!" I said. "That's right up my alley." Getting real has always been the good news to me. As you've learned by now, fake things like acrylic fingernails and borrowed personalities have a way of backfiring on me and attracting pies. I have fretted over how to present myself at many business meetings; fortunately, I always decide I might as well just dress like myself and be who I am because no matter how I look, the minute I open my mouth I will reveal myself. I don't hide well. Not even behind designer clothes, which I don't own anyway. My favorite dress-up outfit, depending on the occasion, is one of two ensembles: a two-piece denim top and skirt (big earrings dress it up) or a green skirt with a jacket that has fringe hanging all over it. People either love this latter look or don't "get" it. I don't care. It's cool. Really cool. And I feel good in it. I have determined that these outfits look like who I am, whatever that means. Perhaps next year my uniforms will be different, but for now they suit me just fine.

Since I would be speaking for three sessions at the Kansas retreat, I broke the theme down into "Unveiling," "Filling" and "Passing It On." The opening talk would be presented Friday night, the next would be given on Saturday morning, and the third on Saturday afternoon just before the close.

Since about 130 women would have to listen to me for a total of nearly three hours, I decided I should be not only interesting but also entertaining during the first session. After all, it would be the end of the work week. The retreatants would be tired; most of them would have driven over an hour to arrive at the site. I didn't want them to listen to my first five minutes and decide this retreat was the biggest mistake they had ever made and they would probably die from terminal boredom; nor did I want them nodding off while I spoke. I wanted them to be glad they were there, get excited about the message and believe they were going to have fun.

Jane filled me in on the committee's plans for the opening agenda and some of the details for the rest of the weekend. It sounded wonderful. Singing, icebreakers, snacks (always a favorite with me) . . . The committee would make all my travel arrangements; all I had to do was arrive and deliver.

I had several months to prepare for the retreat, so I did a lot of reading. Then I began to put the first talk togetheɪ, keeping in mind it should be lively. Introduction: Tell about me. Wife, blah blah blah. Mother, blah blah blah. Writer, blah blah blah. Speaker . . . you get the idea.

Your sister in Christ. A child of God. One who knows God loves her. One of you.

The next nineteen hours or so hold quite the journey for us. We're going to peel away some of our masks, empty, slow down, let the Lord fill us with his goodness and learn how to let his mercy and love flow through us to one another.

We're going to unveil ourselves, be still and know that he is God, then pass on the blessing.

We're going to find out that veils, masks and façades don't protect us, they weigh us down. We'll see just how deep the layers we hide behind are and hope we don't need to call in sand blasters and tow trucks and excavators to haul off all the protective and phony stuff in order to get to our cores.

By the end of this retreat, I hope, we're going to reveal to one another a little more of just who we are. And who we are is God's workmanship. It says so in Ephesians 2:10. "For we are his workmanship, created in Christ Jesus for good works, which God prepared beforehand, that we should walk in them" (NASB).

We're gonna wonder just why we thought draping his workmanship with our masks would make us more appealing and acceptable, especially since he tells us that his power is perfected in our weakness. Paul went so far as to say he gladly boasted about his weaknesses.

We're going to ponder the fact that covering a light with layers of anything only causes it to grow dim, and smolder, and perhaps even flicker out. We're going to become a bellows to one another, fanning our faint embers that so badly need attention and acceptance.

We're going to realize that judging by appearances not only is sinful but can be flat-out misleading. We're going to be surprised, perhaps, not only at who we are, but also at who we're really sitting next to.

We're going to have a good time.

And then, at this very point, a wild and wonderful idea interrupted my speech-writing preparations, sailing in on wings of grace. I should veil my face with something when I entered so my hearers wouldn't be judging me by my hairdo and makeup.

I would let them know that this was an outward symbol of the veils we hide ourselves behind. Yes! Great visual display. I would say, "I want you, for now, to work at seeing past my exterior. I'd like for you to listen to me and try to see me through the eyes of your heart."

This was inspired! I called Jane to ask her if she thought appearing with a veiled face would be too shocking for the women of the Bible church. She said no and assured me that she, too, thought it was a wonderful idea.

I rolled with it, heading for a fabric store. I raced around in there for about a half-hour, looking for just the right veil material. It had to be dark enough to hide me but see-through enough that I could see my notes. I love purple and finally decided on a dark, sheer purple fabric. I would figure out how to drape it at home.

After trying several different wraps, I finally realized that the fabric was all wrong. When the least little fold formed in it, the double layer became too opaque to allow me to see my notes. It also wasn't porous enough to let in air, and I began to suffocate behind my own inspired idea. Back to the drawing board.

After several trials and errors, I hit upon the idea of trying to find a wedding veil in a resale shop. Even more symbolism: after all, the church is Christ's bride. But all the veils I found exceeded my budget because most couldn't be separated from the gowns.

Brainstorm! I remembered that when I was a child I used to wear a half-slip on my head when I played bride. The elastic waistband went around my head like a headband. I would pull half of the slip over my head and in front of my face before I was "married." I ran to my dresser drawer to see if I had kept any of those fluffy, sheer slips. Yes! Of course I had. That's why my underwear drawer never closes right.

Soon I realized that I would have to keep the veil short and find a way to keep it away from my eyes. As with the purple material, folds caused blindness, and the slip had lots of ruffles. I found an old flowered baseball-type hat that we'd received free in a long-ago McDonald's promotion. It jimmy-rigged perfectly. Brilliant!

I went to the retreat.

As I hid my veiled self in a little room and prayed during the opening announcements and icebreakers, I felt more assured than ever that this was a good idea. When I realized it was just about time for me to make my entrance, I stepped outside the little room and waited around the corner of the lecture hall.

Suddenly it hit me.

I was about to address 130 women who had paid good money for this weekend, and here I stood with a slip on my head. I mentally raced through my notes, trying to figure out how much improvising would have to be done if I chucked my costume. I had been worried that women would be nodding off and dying of boredom, but instead they would probably be running for shelter, wondering just what kind of crazy wacko pervert the committee had stuck them with!

No time. I was on. I pushed through the agonizing thoughts and stepped out the door to face my audience, my face covered with a 1960s half-slip that was held in place by a flowered baseball cap.

Was it effective? Yes. Was it funny? Yes. Did I ultimately have fun with this inspiration? Yes. Did anyone have me hauled away? No.

Why did I tell this story? Because not long after I got a thirst to be the humble person that Christ calls me to be, and to write about humility, some powerful fears swept through me, even beyond the who-was-I-to-dare question. This slip-on-my-head story, as I will reveal in a moment, contains a profound lesson about those fears.

My fears went something like this. I am a fun-loving, somewhat devilish kind of gal. Would finding true humility bag my fun? Would my sense of humor evaporate? Would I still be the woman my husband married? Does he even want me to be? Would I have to stop wearing lip gloss? Would my friends still invite me to do lunch? What if I discovered that earrings were out for the humble?

Yikes!

Did truly humble people go around wearing serious-to-gloomy faces because humility is a serious business? Would I have to write for the rest of my life for free and never use a byline again so as not to display pride over my God-given ideas?

Was there fun after humility?

The questions nearly drove me mad for a while. There seemed to be no way to answer them other than to jump in with both feet and find out. Fortunately, God is good and some of the answers have come; you've already read them. Scripture and the works of some great writers have yielded some truths that I would have probably never discovered had I not been thirsting for humility.

Contrary to what you may be thinking, it was true humility that allowed me to wear a flowered baseball cap and a 1960s half-slip on my head (and freed me to indulge in a pie-eating contest). When I had no thoughts of self and appearances, when I was empty and allowing God's creativity to work in and through me, a great visual aid came to mind. In fact, I myself became a visual aid.

The moment I considered only self, I suddenly stood like an idiot wearing a slip on her head (and a pie-filled mouth). Pride said—no, screamed—"You look totally ridiculous and are making a fool of yourself!" Humility whispered, "Christ rode on a donkey." Pride ordered, "Rip that thing off your head and walk in there like a normal person." Humility encouraged, "You are my workmanship. You have committed your work to me, and I say the message matters more than appearances. After all, isn't that what you're here talking about? You say you believe we shouldn't judge by appearances. Do you really believe what you say?"

I've come to an amazing discovery: there's more fun, genuine Spirit-induced fun, with humility than without it. When we are truly humbled, we empty of us and get filled with God, and God never gets embarrassed. God is sovereign. God is faithful. God is unwavering love. We just have to remember to leave the reins in his hands.

This discovery was also made a long time ago, however, by none other than Peter. When he didn't think about walking on water, he could! Now am I tempted to leave my post up at the lake and walk straight into or onto the now-thawed-but-incredibly-cold water? Not just yet. But other kinds of fun seem to be very much in order.

Fun almost always emerges when creativity is allowed to romp. It's too bad self gets in the way of allowing the Creator to create in us. Madeleine L'Engle says:

> All children are artists, and it is an indictment of our culture that so many of them lose their creativity, their unfettered imaginations, as they grow older. But they start off without self-consciousness as they paint their purple flowers, their anatomically impossible people, their thunderous, sulphurous skies. They don't worry that they may not be as good as Di Chirico or Bracque; they know intuitively

that it is folly to make comparisons, and they go ahead and say what they want to say. . . .

So what happens? Why do we lose our wonderful, racketty creativity? What corrupts us?

She goes on to say that we are corrupted by the "dirty devices of the world," quoting Thomas Traherne. She says much of her adult life "has been spent in trying to overcome this corruption . . . which would dull our imaginations, cut away our creativity. So it is only with the conscious-unselfconsciousness of a child that I can think about theories of aesthetics, or art, particularly as these touch upon my questions about life and love and God."[1]

I agree. And so do the Scriptures. "I tell you the truth, unless you change and become like little children, you will never enter the kingdom of heaven. Therefore, whoever humbles himself like this child is the greatest in the kingdom of heaven" (Mt 18:3-4).

Children are very honest, free, spontaneous and not concerned with appearances—until the world trains them to be. Children love to have fun. Their laughter is never contained. Once again I envision the flute player sauntering through the woods. Unselfconscious. Beaming. Childlike in his zeal and joy.

If we are filled with living waters—and we are if we have asked to be—let's dip in with a big dipper and see what comes out. We may be surprised what the Father has already filled us with. What wondrous ideas. What new and inspired notions. You, too, might suddenly have a desire to wear a slip on your head!

Never mind. I got carried away. But do open yourself to

become empty and discover what God has filled you with. What he has already done. "We are all more than we know, and that wondrous reality, that wholeness, holiness, is there for all of us, not the qualified only."[2]

Paul Thigpen says, "To a great extent, I suspect, the living water probably takes the shape of the vessel it fills. Each temperament provides its own lovely form for containing and pouring forth the beauty of His joy."[3] What an absolutely freeing thought that I am free to be me. He created this fun-loving vessel.

Don't misunderstand: I know I need wisdom and temperance, but he is my Creator. I am in him, he in me—and so is his creative ability.

Free to be me. An individual. God's workmanship. Designed by him. Filled with his living waters. Each of us is a unique expression of God, ministering to others in wonderful and marvelous ways. A giant of a man talking to me quietly at the top of a garbage mound. A woman delivering Gummy Bear Boogers to make me laugh. Another person writing as only he can write about grace awakening. Still other expressions of God sharing their lake home. Each ministering to me in his or her special way as I, in turn, hope I minister to them.

Which brings us back to unveiling. The Spirit uncovers what we mistakenly think needs to be covered. Only unveiling enables us to reflect his glory (one of my favorite verses again—2 Cor 3:18), and only an act of complete humility and trust will dare to unveil.

We need to stop comparing ourselves with one another. If I compared my writing skills to those of the greats, I'd never put a word on paper. But I am God's workmanship. He is my

Creator. He has given me my own voice, style and sense of humor. It would be sinful for me to not trust him on this, to lapse into fear and denial and refuse to serve the customized gift he has given me.

I am the One and Only Char the Star. I like to have fun. I hope I am funny, at least some of the time. Laughter is healing medicine. And so is a cheerful heart (Prov 17:22). Remember, what's bubbling inside us erupts out of us, and who doesn't like to be given a cup of joy served by an overflowing friend? Or by fairies dancing in the woods.

Chuck Swindoll quotes a wise rabbinical maxim: "A man will have to give an account on the judgment day for every good thing which he might have enjoyed, and did not."[4] How carelessly we dismiss opportunities to hug and be hugged, to sing and to listen, to simply sit in wonder of God's rich, rich creation. God richly provides us with everything for our enjoyment (1 Tim 6:17). What a pity we honestly believe ourselves too busy to drink it all in. How sinful we've become on our pride-filled treadmills. What a shame Christ gives us so much—"Ask and you will receive, and your joy will be complete" (Jn 16:24)—and we say we're too busy to bother.

Is there fun after humility? There'd better be. Otherwise we've really missed the point.

George MacDonald: "It is the Heart that is not yet sure of its God that is afraid to laugh in His presence."[5]

Madeleine L'Engle: "We can best take ourselves seriously if we are free to laugh at ourselves, and to enjoy the laughter of God and his angels."[6]

Being able to laugh at our own blunders and often pie-smeared selves is truly a blessing. Even though some of the stories in this book are absolutely humiliating, I've had great fun telling them. Yes, it's fun to laugh at ourselves. And it's fun to laugh along with others (definitely different from laughing *at* others) as they unveil and reveal their moments of mishaps. In their doing so we see ourselves and learn that we all fall short.

Is there fun after humility? There's fun in the midst of it. Fun, healing and unending discoveries about God and his magnificence.

10

The Resting Place

WHEN my friend Donna shared her story about illness and teaching and coping, her anguish, triumphs and honesty revealed a very important truth. And she, too, used the word *surrender,* although that is not the truth I want to highlight at the moment.

"Humility is a surrender," she said. "When I come to the very edge of what I can tolerate, I have said to myself, 'I can't take this. I can't do this any more. It is not worth the struggle.' And then—not that it is anything I do; this could very well simply be God—it is almost as though God is saying,

'You're right. You can't take any more. You are at your wit's end. Why don't you try my way for a while?'

"Or something happens that gives you an inkling that your struggle has had something worthwhile in it. Then you can sit back and say, 'I am doing what I need to do, and I am where I need to be to grow.' I think a lot of growth comes through humility because I think it is only when you absolutely can't take any more of where you are going that you grow! These times that are very tense and very hard to live through—it's then that you see beyond yourself. That doesn't mean you have to give in to it. I wouldn't want a God who would require that."

Donna's words struck me as truth during the interview, during my transcription and again as I put them into the pages of this book: I wouldn't want a God who would require relinquishment either. I wouldn't want a God who forced obedience upon me. I would be his puppet, his beaten and helpless slave; he would be my dictator.

But great is the God who gives this free, undeserved gift. Great is he who loves us so much that he allows us to reject the gift. Magnificent is the One who waits and waits while we pridefully try so long to hang on. Wonderful of wonderfuls is the moment when, humbly, we let go and God fills us with more than we can imagine.

Humility: the resting place, not the place of forced compliance.

* * *

On this April morning, the trees have tiny buds that cling to life, even though the sunshine of the past few days has been mingled with snow showers. Just as I raise my eyes to drink in this sign of hope, an eagle soars over the white-capped waters of the lake. From right to left he soars majestically, then flaps his powerful wings.

> Do you not know?
>> Have you not heard?
> The LORD is the everlasting God,
>> the Creator of the ends of the earth.
> He will not grow tired or weary,
>> and his understanding no one can fathom.
> He gives strength to the weary
>> and increases the power of the weak.
> Even youths grow tired and weary,
>> and young men stumble and fall;
> but those who hope in the LORD
>> will renew their strength.
> They will soar on wings like eagles;
>> they will run and not grow weary,
>> they will walk and not be faint.
> (Is 40:28-31)

> Praise the Lord, O my soul . . .
> who satisfies your desires with good things
>> so that your youth is renewed like the eagle's.
> (Ps 103:1-5)

God is good. God is more than we can ever imagine. Like the eagle, we are his workmanship. We are more than we can ever imagine.

"But I still commit sins. Doesn't that make me a sinner?"

. . . There is only one way to determine your identity that cannot be shaken, one foundation that cannot be taken away from you: "I am a child of God." . . . Being made into a new creation does not refer to your behavior; it refers to your identity.[1]

My behavior or my shortcomings or thousands of pies cannot keep me from God's love. "For I am convinced that there is nothing in death or life, in the realm of spirits or superhuman powers, in the world as it is or the world as it shall be, in the forces of the universe, in heights or depths—nothing in all creation that can separate us from the love of God in Christ Jesus our Lord" (Rom 8:38-39 REB).

And so we are without excuse if we refuse humility, refuse to surrender ourselves to God's utmost for our lives. For pride misses the best. Only humility will allow God's loving, warm bath of cleansing while we stand convicted and covered with pies, needing to be made whiter than snow. Only when we understand that he chose us and loved us and knit us together in our mother's womb long before we ever heard of him will we begin to get a glimpse of this awesome gift. We were chosen by him. Just as John and Beth were chosen to receive Michelle. Before they even knew she existed, they had been chosen.

The sweet fruits of humility become the sweet fruits of the Spirit when we surrender and enable Christ to take over. Humble pie becomes a holy feast. And in turn, God is glorified by this, "that you bear much fruit, showing yourselves to be my disciples" (Jn 15:8).

Step seven in the Twelve-Step program is to humbly ask God to remove your shortcomings. In *Hunger for Healing:*

The Twelve Steps as a Classic Model for Christian Spiritual Growth, J. Keith Miller says that

the biggest change the humility of Step Seven brings is in our relationship with God. He is no longer the "helper" who helps us get our agenda back on track so we can accomplish what we want. He is the "owner of the business," and we are trainee employees, learning the business and our part in it one day at a time.

As time goes by we may relax and begin to recognize the God-given aptitudes that we have never let ourselves see fully for fear we might fail.

God can release us to use the freedom and creative power he put in us because we do not have our hands tied up in efforts to control him, his people, and the world he made for us all.[2]

Humility is release from the burden of having to carry the world ourselves. That's not our job anyway, it's God's. Humility knows that. Humility is, indeed, freedom and a place of rest.

"Jacob was a reed," wrote Noah ben Shea, "and the breath of God blew through Jacob, made music of him."[3] Like the flutist in the arboretum, who was free to let the breath of God blow through him—and that breath, that music, enabled even Char the Star to dance with fairies.

* * *

A couple of years ago I took a trip to Oregon to visit my good friend Mary. For two days we rented a condominium in Cannon Beach, right on the ocean. Mary and I shared many intimate thoughts and much laughter; we have a rich history together. The second afternoon of our stay, however,

I rolled up my pant legs, put on my jacket to ward off the fall winds and took a long stroll on the beach alone. There were things I wanted to talk to God about.

I was very aware of the smallness of self against the crashing vastness of God's ocean. The cool water swirled around my toes, tickling them as the remnants of the waves backwashed out away from me and pulled some of the sand from beneath my feet. Ever so gently, grain by grain, the sand loosed and lowered me into God's earth. It was so gentle; yet I knew that death hovered near should I wade out and get caught in the undertow of one of the huge breakers. Once when I was a child I was pulled under by the sea's force. Tossed and turned and choking, my body was finally deposited on the shore by the grace of God. Yes, I know the ocean's power.

In the stretching shadows of the late of day, I finally gave in to my unrest and approached God's throne. Although God had made it clear that I had not gotten a book contract and Mary Beth had not gotten a child with cancer because either of us deserved it, I still struggled with a small, stubborn sense of guilt. Exactly who was I and where was God taking me? Needing peace in this troubled corner of my heart, I stopped walking and called aloud toward the ocean, "Lord, who do you say that I am? You need to tell me. *Who do you say that I am?*" Tears and a sense of urgency caused my voice to rise and compete with the great roar before me. It did not seem an unfair question; even Christ had asked it of his disciples (Mt 16:15). Of course that was their test, not his. But his words coming out of my mouth did not seem inappropriate.

And then I heard his voice. Clearly his voice boomed in my head. "I AM," was all he said.

"Lord, that's not what I asked you. Who do you say that *I* am?" The words choked out of me, though I feared to be so bold as to answer back. To holler back to a God who was clearly talking to me. But Jacob wrestled with an angel an entire night until the angel blessed him, so I took a deep breath and unabashedly repeated my question: "Lord, that is not what I asked you. Who do you say that I am?"

"I AM. That is all you need to know." This came with a tone of finality; and then his voice was silent. All I could hear now were the crashing, thunderous waves.

I stood staring at the gray horizon as it disappeared and reappeared between swells. Weeping. Finally understanding that he was all. He was all of me. He was all I needed to know, although I could never know all of him.

Moses once asked God, "Who am I, that I should go to Pharaoh and bring the Israelites out of Egypt?"

And God said, "I will be with you" (Ex 3:11-12). It was all Moses needed to know. But he still asked more.

Moses said to God, "Suppose I go to the Israelites and say to them, 'The God of your fathers has sent me to you,' and they ask me, 'What is his name?' Then what shall I tell them?"

God said to Moses, "I AM WHO I AM. This is what you are to say to the Israelites: 'I AM has sent me to you.' " (vv. 13-14)

I AM. He is everything. He is all we need to know. He is everything and everything is his, including the parts of me I pridefully and stubbornly try so hard to hang on to.

* * *

Joyce's friend invited her to a retreat. Joyce didn't really want to go, but her friend told her she was going, and that was that. Friends are often the voice of God.

The speaker based his presentation on the love texts from 1 Corinthians. Joyce wasn't in a very good mood; life had not been happy lately. Besides that, she already knew this stuff. "Yeah yeah yeah," she thought as he talked.

And then he began to talk about forgiveness. Joyce's "yeah yeah yeahs" continued, blocking out some of what he was saying. But a voice inside her said, "Be still and listen!"

Joyce did not ignore the strong voice of God. She listened, and suddenly something in her began to well up as he spoke—directly to her soul. She became convicted that what was wrong with her life was a lack of forgiveness.

Three people. It was immediately clear to her that there were three people she needed to forgive. The emotions that came with this revelation were so strong that she wept, felt ill and could not even eat lunch. But she also humbly surrendered to God's voice.

Later, Joyce went off by herself to a river that ran through the conference grounds. She picked up three twigs. One at a time she dropped them in the river, allowing the current to carry them away—and her unforgiveness with them.

One twig became stuck. "Turn away. Don't look!" the voice said. And so Joyce obediently turned away. When she finally looked again, the twig was gone. All three twigs had been washed away. All three people had been forgiven.

Oh the resting place when one lets go of anger and forgives. Only a willing, humble spirit can truly let go of wounds and allow God's grace to heal, replacing the dark recesses with light.

Washed. Cleansed. Forgiven. Forgiving. Rest.

* * *

I had never read *Anne of Green Gables*. I first experienced the story on public television. In the middle of the delightful tale, Anne, a very dramatic young woman, is carrying on about her despair. Marilla, played by Colleen Dewhurst, stops dead in her tracks on the way up the stairs, turns to face Anne and says, "To despair is to turn your back on God."

One minute I'm watching a fun little program; the next minute I'm rocked by truth and power.

To despair is to choose darkness. To despair is to turn away from God's loving arms. To hope and trust and allow yourself to be enfolded by his love is the resting place. Grace. God's love, by the pure gift of grace, is always close.

Pride leads to despair. Dependence upon self and an unwillingness to yield to help, even God's, leads to despair. How exhausting. And what a blessed resting place to be able to fall weeping into his arms and say, "Father, I need you." And he always says, "Yes, my child, I am here. I've been waiting. Let me comfort you."

Rest comes from releasing your plans to Him and receiving His plans. Rest comes from keeping your eyes fixed upon Him instead of your circumstances. Rest comes from ceasing to live for self and living in Him.

Rest will come, not from things or people, not from the removal of circumstances; rest will come from Him.[4]

Not that you'll never have problems again. "I have told you these things, so that in me you may have peace. In this world you will have trouble. But take heart! I have overcome the world" (Jn 16:33).

But God does not forcefully overcome our prideful selves. Surrender is our choice. He does wing a few pies in there. Just to get our attention. Just to enlighten us to the fact that there is something we need to let go of. Something that needs changing in us. Something we need to let him handle. He wants us to turn it over to him and enter his resting place.

"Stop dwelling on past events and brooding over days gone by. I am about to do something new; this moment it will unfold. Can you not perceive it?" (Is 43:18-19 REB).

* * *

Humility brings not only rest but confidence as well. Let me share with you excerpts from a dialogue between Cornel West and Bell Hooks—Christian African-American scholars who are concerned to promote God's justice.

BH: What is the place of humility in the lives of those of us who would be leaders? You say that "to be humble is to be so sure of one's self and one's mission that one can forgo calling excessive attention to one's self and status. And even more pointedly, to be humble is to revel in the accomplishment or potential of others. . . ."

CW: Humility means two things.

One, a capacity for self-criticism. . . .

The second feature is allowing others to shine, affirming others, empowering and enabling others. Those who lack humility are dogmatic and egotistical. That masks a deep sense of insecurity. They fear the success of others at the expense of their own fame and glory. . . .

Humility requires maturity.[5]

Martin Luther King Jr. was such an example of this kind of leader, West says. In his humble leadership, King, filled with

God's power, affected the course of history. He was not out to draw attention to himself; his business was to call attention to the needs of God's people. Not only did he accomplish this magnificently, but he brought hope and lifted up many and encouraged many on the way.

Humility and confidence in God's power within enables you to boldly tackle the job the Lord has given you. More than that, humility transcends you. Humility helps enlighten and enable those whom you love. Those whom God's power is touching through you.

* * *

The Scriptures give us this calling: "Shine like stars in the universe as you hold out the word of life" (Phil 2:15-16). Quite a heavenly commission. Madeleine L'Engle says, "We can be humble only when we know that we are God's children, of infinite value, and eternally loved."[6]

Infinitely treasured. Eternal. Shining.

* * *

"Jacob, what are the limits of a man?"

"Ask the man!" said Jacob, without losing his pace.

"And what if the man acknowledges no limits?"

"Then you've discovered his."

"But," the student persisted, "what then is the route to wisdom?"

"Humility!" came the reply.

"How long is the route?"

And Jacob answered, "I don't know."[7]

Jacob the Baker says he does not know how long the route to humility is. I believe it is as close as surrender, and I beam when I say it, like a beacon in the cosmos.

Only through the eyes of humility—complete awareness of and dependence on God's awesome, faithful love for me—do I gratefully learn that I am of infinite value, eternally loved and shining like a star. Char the Star.

To Contact Charlene

Charlene Ann Baumbich is an author, speaker, and humorist who loves to hear *back* from people. If you'd like to do one or more of the following...

- contact Charlene about speaking
- desire to be added to her mailing list
- would like to receive an order blank offering Charlene's current book and audio tape selection and prices
- Or just have a comment:

       Charlene Ann Baumbich
       22W 371 Second Street
       Glen Ellyn, Illinois 60137

       Phone: (630) 858-1091
       Fax: (630) 858-1094
       Email: Charstar1@Juno.com

Notes

Preface: Open to the Shining
[1]Madeleine L'Engle, *Walking on Water: Reflections on Faith and Art* (Wheaton, Ill.: Harold Shaw, 1980), p. 62.
[2]Reuben Welch, *We Really Do Need Each Other* (Nashville: Generoux Nelson, 1982), p. 67.

Chapter 1: The Thirst
[1]Andrew Murray, *Humility* (Springfield, Penn.: Whitaker House, 1982), p. 6.

Chapter 2: What Humility Is Not
[1]Paul Tillich, *The Shaking of the Foundations* (New York: Charles Scribner's Sons, 1966), p. 163.
[2]Bob George, *Classic Christianity* (Eugene, Ore.: Harvest House, 1989), p. 178.
[3]Jim Conway, *Friendship* (Grand Rapids, Mich.: Zondervan, 1989), pp. 36-37.
[4]Charles R. Swindoll, *Simple Faith* (Dallas: Word Books, 1991), p. 145.

Chapter 3: Incentives
[1]Joni Eareckson Tada, *Seeking God* (Brentwood, Tenn.: Wolgemuth & Hyatt, 1991), p. 36.

[2]Bless Your Heart, series 2 (Eden Prairie, Minn.: Heartland Samplers, 1990).

[3]Murray, *Humility,* p. 13.

[4]Charles Stanley, *How to Listen to God* (Nashville: Oliver Nelson, 1985), p. 91.

[5]George, *Classic Christianity,* p. 52.

Chapter 4: Awakenings

[1]Mother Teresa, *Total Surrender,* rev. ed. (Ann Harbor, Mich.: Servant, 1985), pp. 27-28.

[2]Mary Ellen Ashcroft, *Temptations Women Face* (Downers Grove, Ill.: InterVarsity Press, 1991), p. 46.

Chapter 5: The Power Within

[1]Murray, *Humility,* p. 38.

[2]Lloyd John Ogilvie, *Autobiography of God* (Ventura, Calif.: Regal Books, 1979), p. 194.

[3]Charles R. Swindoll, *The Grace Awakening* (Dallas: Word Books, 1990), p. 220.

[4]J. I. Packer, *Knowing God* (Downers Grove, Ill.: InterVarsity Press, 1973), p. 37.

[5]Peggy Benson, *Listening for a God Who Whispers* (Nashville: Generoux Nelson, 1991), pp. 195, 200.

Chapter 6: Does Humility Show?

[1]Donald W. McCullough, *Finding Happiness in the Most Unlikely Places* (Downers Grove, Ill.: InterVarsity Press, 1990), p. 30.

[2]Used by permission, Gary L. Bradshaw.

Chapter 7: The Pie-Slinging Blues

[1]Tada, *Seeking God,* p. 8.

[2]Murray, *Humility,* p. 84.

Chapter 8: Humbling Awe

[1]Thomas Paul Thigpen, *A Reason for Joy* (Colorado Springs, Colo.: NavPress, 1988), pp. 25-26.

[2]Murray, *Humility,* pp. 6, 26.

Chapter 9: Is There Fun After Humility?

[1]L'Engle, *Walking on Water,* pp. 51-52.

[2]Ibid., p. 64.
[3]Thigpen, *A Reason for Joy,* p. 28.
[4]Quoted in Swindoll, *Simple Faith,* p. 146.
[5]Quoted in L'Engle, *Walking on Water,* p. 131.
[6]L'Engle, *Walking on Water,* p. 132.

Chapter 10: The Resting Place
[1]George, *Classic Christianity,* pp. 79, 84, 89.
[2]J. Keith Miller, *Hunger for Healing: The Twelve Steps as a Classic Model for Christian Spiritual Growth* (San Francisco: Harper, 1991), pp. 120-22.
[3]Noah ben Shea, *Jacob the Baker* (New York: Ballantine Books, 1989), p. 7.
[4]Millie Stamm, *Be Still and Know* (Grand Rapids, Mich.: Zondervan, 1978), April 4 entry.
[5]"Friends of Mind," *Other Voices,* March-April 1992, p. 16.
[6]L'Engle, *Walking on Water,* p. 69.
[7]Ben Shea, *Jacob the Baker,* p. 45.